Dick Taylor

BRITISH INFANTRY TANKS

in World War II

KAGERO

British Infantry Tanks in World War II • Dick Taylor • First edition • LUBLIN 2016

 • **ISBN 978-83-65437-12-9**

Editors: **Dick Taylor** • Photo: **Author, Archive of Kagero**
Photo caption: **Dick Taylor** • Color profiles: **Arkadiusz Wróbel** • Cover image: **Arkadiusz Wróbel**
Design: **KAGERO STUDIO, Marcin Wachowicz**

Oficyna Wydawnicza KAGERO
Akacjowa 100, Turka, os. Borek, 20-258 Lublin 62, Poland, phone/fax: (+48) 81 501 21 05
www.kagero.pl • e-mail: kagero@kagero.pl, marketing@kagero.pl
w w w . k a g e r o . p l

The A11E1 prototype as first built in 1936. Although it is clearly similar to the production version, the toothed idlers, low mounted rear drive sprocket and turret design can all be seen here.

Introduction

Before the start of the Second World War, British armoured doctrine was in a terrible muddle. Opinion had been divided between the proponents of the tank who saw it as the weapon of break-in, using it as an infantry support weapon, and those who saw it as the weapon of break-out, using it to restore mobility and to destroy the enemy's forces behind the frontline. In many ways it was a division between those who saw the tank solely through the prism of the experience of the First World War, and those who saw it a decisive weapon for the future. Britain was also conscious of the continuing requirements for imperial policing, in which small tanks and armoured cars had already proved their worth. As a consequence, it was decided that Britain needed three different classes of tanks: Light tanks for the policing role that could also be used for reconnaissance duties in a general war; fast and lightly armoured Cruiser tanks for break-out and exploitation, and heavily armoured but slow Infantry tanks for the break-in.

Unfortunately, what the policy makers had failed to realise was that the use of tanks in a future war would be very different from the experience of WW1: it would prove to be impossible to neatly segregate the battlefield in both time and space to suit the three different types of tanks, and that what was required was a single tank that was heavily armoured enough to support the infantry, but also fast and reliable enough to conduct more mobile operations, including break-out and pursuit. In time – well after the war - this would come to be called the Main Battle Tank, and would be supported by a host of other specialised armoured vehicles, including Armoured Personnel Carriers, reconnaissance tanks, and not least, a range of engineering variants. It should be noted at this point that Germany started the war with a similar method of classifying tanks, but realised quicker than Britain that the artificial division was unhelpful on the battlefield and crucially, was faster and more successful at doing something about it.

It can of course be argued that in Britain the technology of 1939 was not capable of producing such a tank, but as it was not attempted until around 1943, it is difficult to know for certain. What is clear is that Britain went to war with a small fleet of different tanks divided artificially into the three very separate classes, and this book will look at one of those classes, the Infantry Tank. In particular, whilst mentioning briefly some of the variants and failed designs in that class, we shall concentrate on the four main types that saw battlefield service as Infantry tanks (sometimes called I-Tanks): the Matilda I, the Matilda II, the Valentine, and the Churchill. These were known officially as the Infantry Tanks Marks I to IV respectively, and this designation reflects the order in which they were designed, produced, and entered service. They were the basis of many experimental and specialised variants, but due to space considerations we shall concern ourselves here mainly with the major tank versions.

Despite the artificial compartmentalisation of British tanks that was eventually to be exposed as a dreadful mistake, there is no doubt that all these tanks, and particularly the last three, performed sterling service in different ways during the conflict; all saw combat, which is more than can be said for many of the designs produced in the Cruiser class, particularly the Covenanter and Cavalier. None were without their faults, and the crews seem to have operated them with a mixture of admiration and exasperation, but all contributed to final victory and are thus deserving of recognition. It should be noted that this book is intended to serve as a "primer", and space precludes an expert discussion on every aspect of every mark of each tank discussed – some 25 in all! We shall start with the first, least known and least successful of the four, the Infantry Tank Mark 1 or Matilda.

A11 Infantry Tank Mk I Matilda

Once the British army had decided that it needed a new type of tank to support the infantry it was faced with a seemingly insurmountable problem: there was virtually no money with which to design, develop, and then produce it. What rearmament money was available was prioritised to the RAF and then the Royal Navy, with the Army a distant third. And what small sums were given to the Army had to be spread around all of its arms and services, and so it became clear that any new tank would have to be built to a very limited budget, which in turn would limit its specification and therefore its combat capability. Added to this was the problem that Britain only possessed one armaments firm experienced in designing and making tanks: Vickers-Armstrong.

Now bearing the civilian registration CMM880, the prototype has had the rear sprocket raised and the front idler wheel changed for a plain type, and has had square headlamps fitted to the hull sides.

A poor quality image, but which shows one of the first batch of production tanks being inspected by foreign VIPs. The name DEVIL identifies it as belonging to 4RTC, the first unit to receive the type.

4RTR tanks on their way to northern France in the winter of 1939; the crews are still wearing the old style service dress, as battledress had not yet been issued.

HMH799 also bore the military registration T3444 and was used by both 4RTR and 7RTR in 1940. The white squares are the hastily-applied BEF recognition symbols.

HMH830 was also registered as T3475, and belonged to 7RTR where she was named GIGGLE, the name being painted in front of the driver's visor and also on the right rear trackguard. The A Squadron triangle is marked in solid white on the turret rear, and she carries the newly-applied BEF white recognition squares painted on the hull front and sides.

HMH812 left UK for France on 29th September 1939, and the small size of the tank meant it was easily transportable by rail, a useful attribute.

In 1934 suggestions were put forward that the new I-Tank required might take one of two forms. The first was a small and "inconspicuous" tank armed with a machine-gun, basically nothing more than a (not very) mobile MG pillbox. The other was a larger tank carrying a gun. Due to the lack of funds the first option was the only one that had a chance of seeing the light of day, and in October 1935, the chief designer for Vickers, Sir John Carden, produced a sketch and outline specification for a two-man tank to meet this need. The overriding characteristic was to be cheapness – there was no point in adding on bells and whistles if they made it unaffordable. Carden suggested that it might be produced for under £15,000 (still a large sum) by keeping it simple and using existing technologies and components wherever possible. (As it was it came out at around £6000 per tank). At a meeting with the Assistant Director of Mechanisation the project was given the Vickers codename Matilda. (The long-standing story is that the tank was named after a cartoon duck, which it resembled when moving. However, the first known appearance of the Disney "Matilda the Duck" was not until well after WW2 so that story can be put to bed!)

The other characteristics suggested were sketchy but in the event accurate. It was to be armed with a .303 MG with 3000 rounds of ammunition, and would be capable of 5 MPH, with 8MPH to be "hoped for"! (In the event the official top speed was 5.8 mph, but when in service the drivers found a way of bypassing the Zenith speed governor in order to make it go at around 11 mph, but it remained a slow vehicle.) Greater speed was not deemed to be necessary as it would only have to keep pace with infantry troops who were advancing cross-country

T5575 GLENLYON of C Sqn 7RTR having been abandoned in May 1940. The tank is of the second type, and has the PTO cover for the Fowler mineplough visible on the open transmission hatch.

Another view of T5575 GLENLYON of 7RTR, abandoned after becoming stuck in a ditch in May 1940. The rear decking has been lifted, showing the housing which tells us that she was one of the tanks able to carry the Fowler mine plough equipment.

An abandoned 4RTR tank being examined by interested German armoured troops in 1940. Some tanks were sent back to Germany for a more extensive analysis, but, unlike many captured vehicles, do not appear to have been converted by the Germans for their use.

T5574 (aka RMY928) being used to support a washing line post-capture! This tank was not one of those used in action, but was part of the reserve fleet held at No 1 Sub-depot, part of No2 Base Ordnance Depot.

and "leaning on the shoulder" of a slow-moving artillery barrage. A range of 60 miles was specified, from 42 gallons of petrol housed in two square 21 gallon tanks, one either side. It was 15' 11" long, and 7' 8" both wide and high.

The crew was to be only two men, the commander in a small cast steel turret, where he would not only command the vehicle but also load and fire the MG. If he was also a Section Commander, he would also co-ordinate the movement of the other two tanks by the use of hand signals or flags, as to keep the cost down wireless (radio) was not to be fitted. However, when the tanks entered service, at least some were fitted with the No 11 set, reducing the internal space and adding to the commander's burden as he had to both use and tune the set – the latter was no mean feat and not an act of war, as to do it he had to lie down in the small space behind the driver on the floor! The provision of radio cost more money but was in line with British doctrine, as it was clearly understood that armoured formations really needed wireless in order to act together and to seize fleeting opportunities. The commander's normal seat was nothing more than a strap slung from either side of the turret walls. The driver sat in a small box compartment at the front of the tank, with a visor above his head which he raised upwards when not in action, allowing him to drive with his head out. Under fire, he would close the visor over his head and look out through either a set of simple vision slits and armoured glass prisms, or through a Vickers tank periscope. Unfortunately, this design meant that if the gun was firing horizontally to the front, the most likely scenario, the armoured jacket for the MG prevented the driver from raising and exiting through his hatch, a dangerous design flaw. Communication was a one-way affair from the commander to the driver using a rudimentary speaking tube; the latter heard the instructions using headsets but could not respond unless he shouted up to his boss!

Mechanically the tank was extremely simple. The engine chosen was an off-the-shelf commercial item, a 70hp Ford V8 Model 79F-6000 driving a four-speed crash gearbox transmission through a rear sprocket, and the suspension was based upon the system employed on the Vickers Mk IV artillery

GARBO was another second type operated by 7RTR. Like many of the vehicles photographed after capture, it does not appear to be damaged so it may have broken down or simply run out of fuel.

tractor (Dragon) which itself derived from the 6 Ton tank of the late 1920s. The armour ranged from a minimum of 10mm to – for the time – an impressive 60mm on the turret and around the hull including the rear, remembering that at this time no-one in Britain was considering much above 30mm as being necessary, as anti-tank guns were in their infancy. The hull was constructed using riveted plates with a bolted nose, and the pointed nose kept the weight down and was also ballistically efficient. The suspension was very exposed to enemy fire or damage by mines, but the tank did have the advantage of being simple to train soldiers on and to operate, and appears to have been fairly reliable, in part because it was so very simple. In order to give it more hitting power, some tanks had the .303" Vickers MMG replaced with the slightly larger .50" heavy version of the gun, and accounts of the tanks in action refer to this weapon being used. Two 4" Smoke Grenade dischargers were also fitted, one either side of the turret.

A prototype called the A11E1 was produced by Vickers in short order and was developed by them during 1936, then in September it was sent to the Mechanisation Experimental Establishment in Surrey for army trials. A11 was the project code, and E1 stood for the first experimental model. Because of the simplicity of the design, and due to the pressing need for tanks, it was accepted for production with only a few modifications, including redesigning the turret, adjusting the rear suspension to raise the rear sprocket and hence the ground clearance, and substituting a plain front idler wheel for the toothed design originally proposed. The first contract was placed in April 1938 for 60 machines. Another 60 were ordered only one month later, and a final batch of 19 in January 1939, bringing the total built to 140. It is probable that this small number built reflected the realisation that the model would be a stop-gap at best, and that larger and more capable I-Tanks were what was required, as we shall see.

Contract	Qty	Registrations (military)	Registrations (civil)	Remarks
T.4349 April 1938	60	T3433 – T3492	HMH788 – HMH847	Completed April 1939
T.5429 May 1938	60	T5551 – T5610	RMY905 – RMY964	Completed February 1940
T.6458 January 1939	19	T8101 – T8119	PMX458 – PMX476	Completed August 1940

The majority of the first batch were of the early model, and were used to equip 4RTC and 7RTC in 1st Army Tank Brigade. The second batch completed the equipping of those two regiments and the remainder started to equip the third regiment, 8RTC, as well as providing spare tanks held by the BEFs Base Ordnance Depots in France, with the remainder going to new armoured units in the UK to assist with AFV training. Although never differentiated as such by the issuing of a Mark number, there were two types of A11 made. The first batch is easily distinguished by the high mounted headlamps on the hull sides. The second type featured modifications to allow a Fowler mineplough kit to be used, and these were distinguished by the addition of a power take-off fixture on the hull rear; this necessitated moving the headlamps forward and lower to get them out of the way of the plough when fitted. The shape of the external stowage bins was also amended, as was the position of the driver's periscope. (The necessity to fit mine ploughs was decided upon once it was realised that some tanks proposed, including the A20 (see below) were vulnerable to mine attack, and therefore it was decided that the already obsolete A11 might be able to usefully plough lanes and routes clear of mines.)

The tank only saw action for a limited period, in the hands of 4th and 7th Battalions Royal Tank Regiment in operations in Belgium and France after the German invasion on May 10th

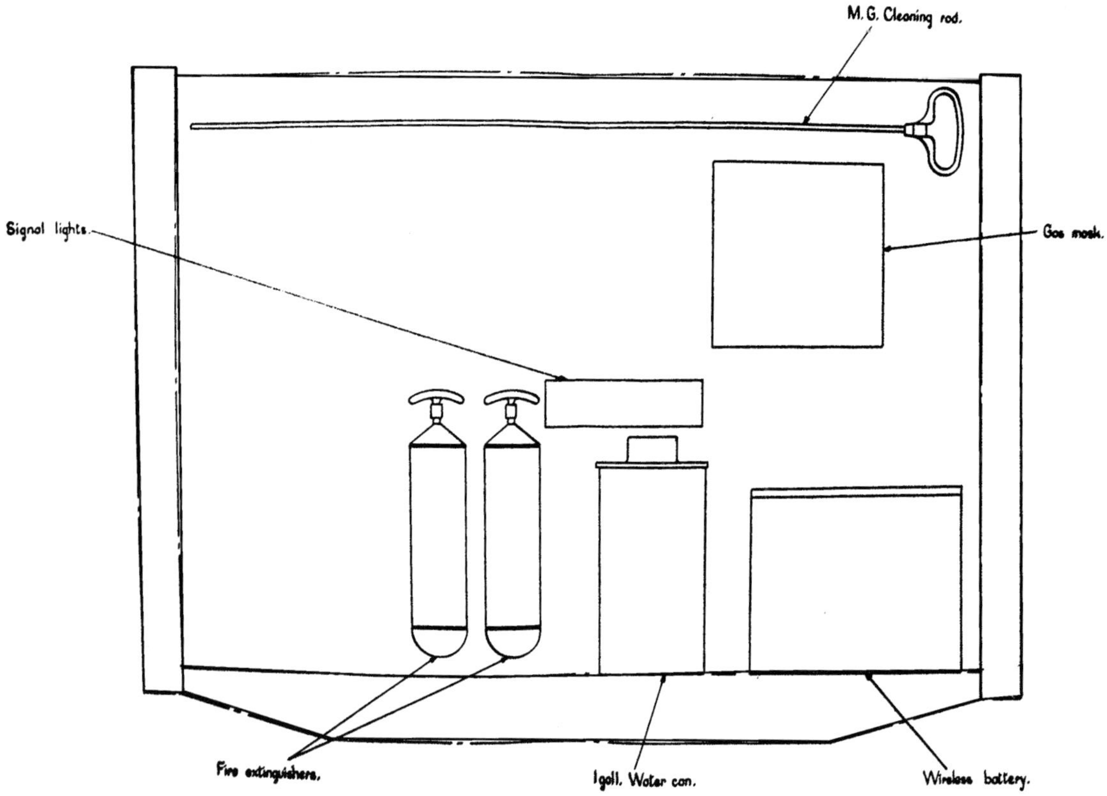

Stowage diagrams taken from the official “stuffing” diagrams used to show crews where tools etc were to be placed.

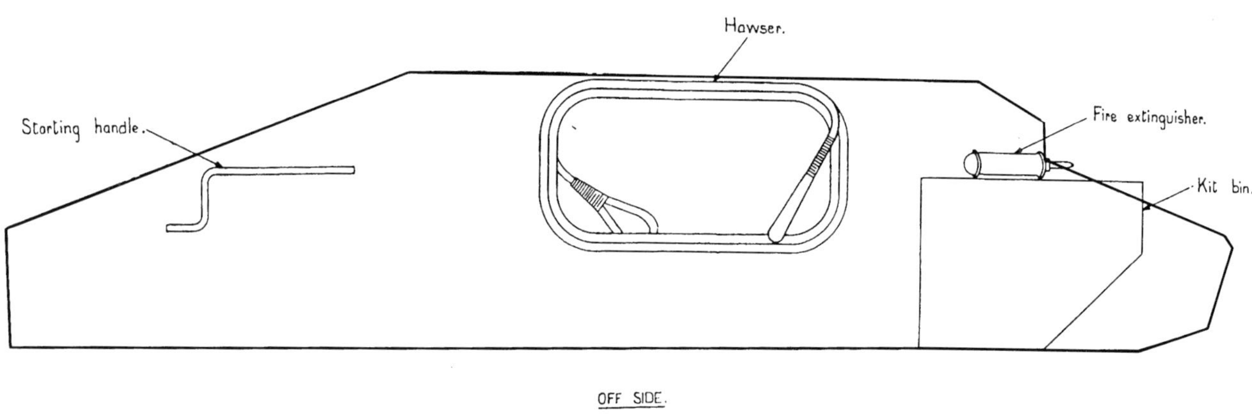

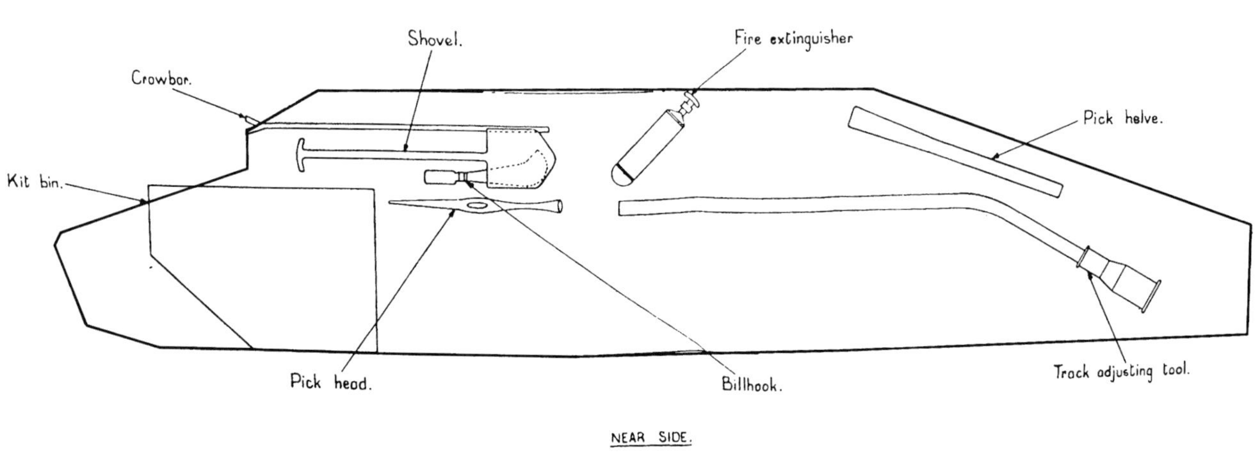

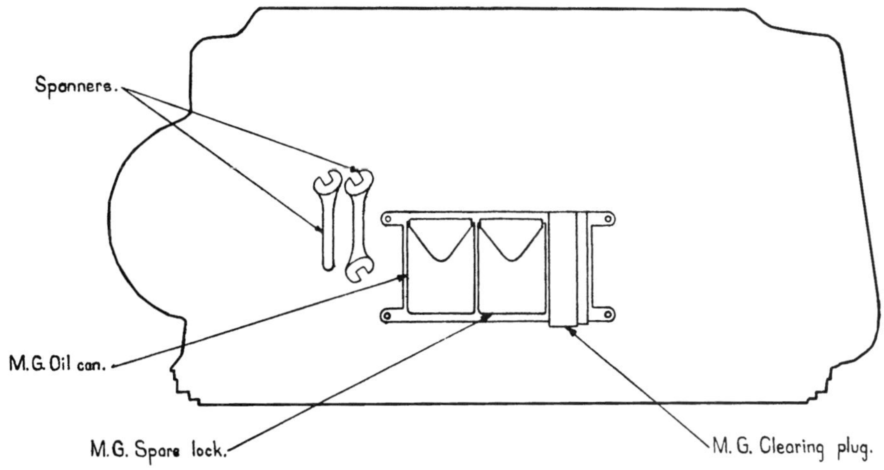
Spanners.
M.G. Oil can.
M.G. Spare lock.
M.G. Clearing plug.

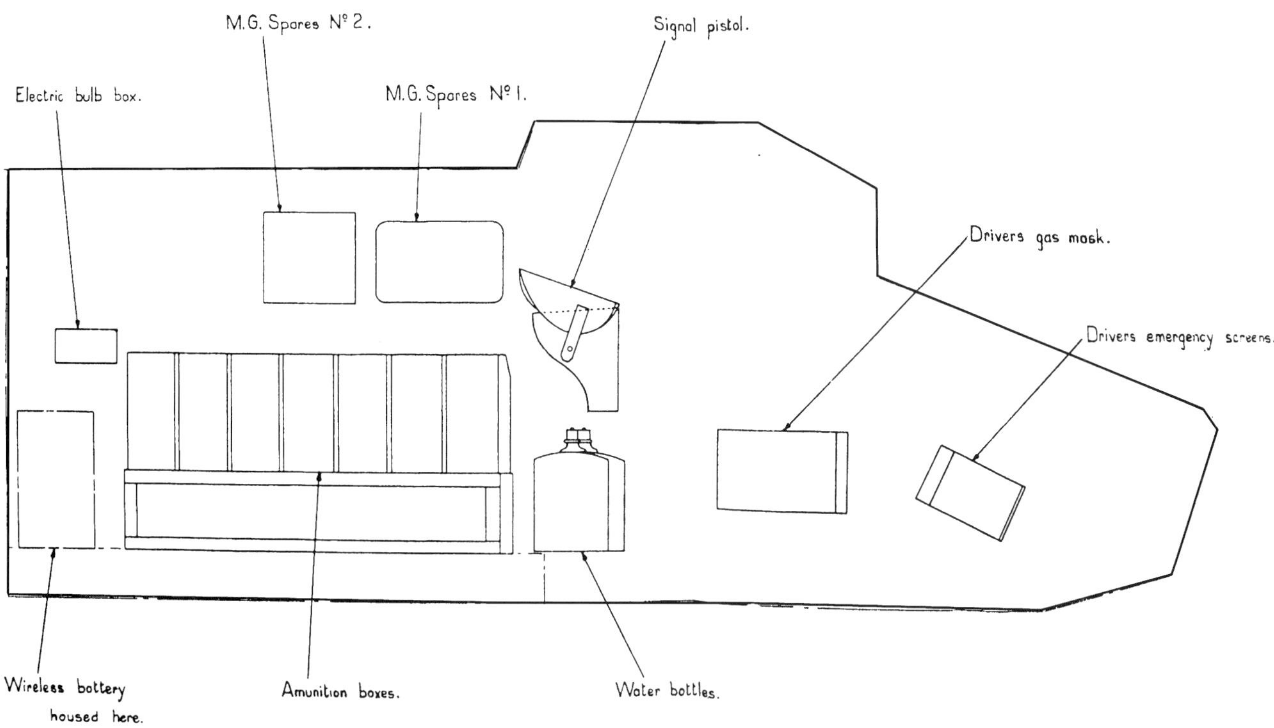
M.G. Spares Nº 2.
Signal pistol.
Electric bulb box.
M.G. Spares Nº 1.
Drivers gas mask.
Drivers emergency screens.
Wireless battery housed here.
Amunition boxes.
Water bottles.

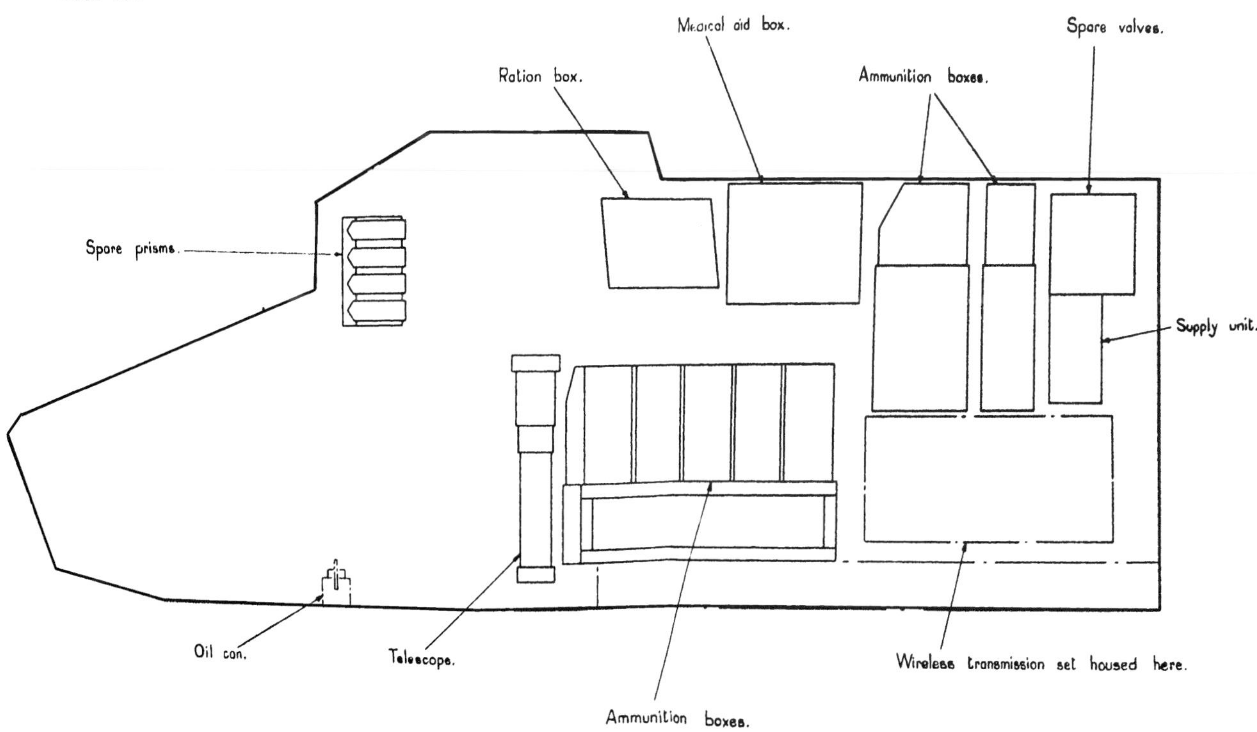
Medical aid box.
Spare valves.
Ration box.
Ammunition boxes.
Spare prisms.
Supply unit.
Oil can.
Telescope.
Wireless transmission set housed here.
Ammunition boxes.

1940. 4RTR were fully equipped with 48 Matilda I, whereas 7RTR operated 27 of the type, in three Sections of three in each of the three Companies; A12s were also used in 7RTR. All of the tanks sent to France were either destroyed or were captured, nearly 100 in all including the ones held in reserve. In their short life they demonstrated that their armour could take fearsome punishment; one tank was hit 14 times by German anti-tank rounds but not penetrated. Members of 4RTR recalled their memories of the A11 during the Arras counter-attack:

> *I distinctly remember SSM "Muscle" Armit with [his] .5" gun just ahead of me getting repeated hits on his tank turret...crossing a railway line [outside Achicour] was tricky, fear of jamming tracks, but was safely negotiated...my driver was finding me targets quicker than I could myself...everyone was firing away briskly and I claimed a motorcycle and sidecar machine-gun outfit...I decided to polish off two lorries parked near where an anti-tank gun was placed. Next thing, a flash and a cloud of smoke. This had been an ammo lorry and its demise also stopped the gun...I could not see a thing as the corn was higher than the driver's visor...suddenly the glass in my driver's visor shattered, we found afterwards that a shell had knocked a rivet clean out of the armour plating...to our great surprise we found that we had come straight into the flank of a German mechanised column...the was a glorious free-for-all. We knocked out quite a lot of their lorries, there were Germans running about all over the place...some of them had a go at jumping on our tanks and I remember that I myself had a German who climbed on the outside of my tank and looked in the periscope, then a neighbouring tank very kindly turned his machine gun on me and that removed my passenger...It's quite an experience seeing guns getting trained on your tank and wondering if the shell is going to come through. Several of our tanks seemed to be burning, but it was caused by sparks as the bullets passed through the non-armoured tool bins which had petrol stores in them, and it was these which caught alight...*

Although never really used in the infantry support role during an offensive against a prepared enemy position for which it was designed, the A11 was thus able to find its place in history when it was used in the famous Arras counter-attack by the two regiments on 21st May 1940, as described above. It should be realised that this was the first indication that the artificial distinction of building tanks according to a pre-conceived role was not workable in war, as the slow and poorly-armed A11s had in fact been used in the role that should have been filled by Cruiser tanks... but that lesson was not learned, nor would it be for a number of years. In the meantime, the British would look to what some people referred to as Matilda Senior, the Infantry Tank Mk II. Production ceased on 2nd August 1940, and the final use of the Matilda I was in the training role within the UK; 18 were operated by the Polish Army training in Scotland from 1940 until 1942, when they were handed in and replaced by more modern types; this probably marks the end of their useful life, at which point the majority would have been scrapped. Three examples, one used as a range target, are on display at the Bovington Tank Museum.

A12 Infantry Tank Mk II Matilda II

It will be remembered that in the mid 1930s the British had really wanted a larger Infantry Tank than the A11, one with a gun. The initial investigation into what would become the A12 tank started in late 1936, but was handicapped by the realisation that the usual port of call for tanks, Vickers-Armstrong, was full to capacity and therefore the army had to find a new manufacturer, one who would be able to both design the tank and then produce it. Not surprisingly, as rearmament was gathering pace, the choice fell to a company that was available, rather than one that was particularly suited to the task. The company with the spare capacity was Vulcan Foundry, located between Manchester and Liverpool, which was given the task in November 1936.

Designing the tank was conducted by the company, who initially were only able to find two draughtsmen to design the tank, although they were later able to increase this to eight. Designing a tank from scratch would be beyond the abilities of most firms, whatever their engineering expertise, and it was only with significant assistance from the Mechanization Board that the tank was produced. Despite all these hindrances, the prototype, known at that stage as Matilda Senior, was designed and built (from mild steel) in a little over a year, and began its trials in spring 1938. As was the custom in those days, a lot of the tank was built first, and only then were drawings produced from the prototype! Despite the potential for disaster the tank turned out to be a sound design and required little in the way of modification before it was put into production. It was quickly realised that Vulcan could not produce sufficient numbers of the tank quickly enough, and five other firms were brought in to build the tank. These were Ruston & Hornsby, the London Midland & Scottish Railway, John Fowlers, North British Locomotives, and Harland & Wolff. Eventually 2920 were built, production ending as late as August 1943 due to supplies of the now-obsolete tank being sent to the USSR and Australia.

A Matilda production line, with at least 14 tanks in various stages of construction visible. British manufacturers did not use the genuine assembly line techniques used in the USA, and relied on skilled workers to make parts fit.

Many Matildas were sent to the USSR via the Arctic convoy system. This propaganda photo purports to show the tank being painted, complete with greeting slogan in Russian. Four of the six workers are female.

Brand new! This Matilda has just been completed and awaits its main armament, which were often not fitted until the tanks arrived at an RAOC depot where they were also kitted out with tools and prepared for issue. Note the single headlamp with blackout mask.

Painted along the side are typical markings showing the maximum fording heights when operating "Flaps open" and Flaps closed". The tank is fitted with the No 19 radio set, identifiable by the two antennae on the turret, and the druid-like auxiliary fuel tank on the rear hull.

Another brand new Matilda, this time the Close Support variant with 3" howitzer, identifiable by the thicker, non-tapered gun barrel. Although capable of firing HE, the British used this weapon as much for creating local smoke screens as delivering fire support.

T6751 was a Matilda II made by Vulcan Foundry and issued to 7RTR on 26th February 1940. She was commanded in France by Sgt Benjamin Doyle who was awarded a Distinguished Conduct Medal for his actions at Arras, knocking out two German batteries and two tanks as well as an 88mm gun. GOOD LUCK fell into German hands more or less intact after being knocked out by another 88mm; note the Vickers MG shroud next to the 2 Pounder barrel and the raised suspension units, she also carried the rear tail-skid.

T6909 GREENOCK was a Mk I Matilda II built by the London Midland and Scottish Railway company, and belonged to C Sqn 7RTR when she was captured in 1940. She also has the raised suspension units to improve the ground clearance and although not clear from this photograph, had a rear tail-skid extension fitted to aid crossing trenches.

As an Infantry support tank, the choice of weapons for the Matilda was somewhat strange. The tank was armed with the 40mm 2 Pounder gun, an excellent weapon which was the best anti-tank gun of its day, and thus capable of protecting the infantry from attacks by enemy tanks. But it was incapable of firing high explosive ammunition (an HE round was made but its explosive content was very small and in any case it was not issued to tank units) and therefore not capable of providing the necessary fire support to infantry attacking a defended objective. Some tanks were designated as CS (Close Support) tanks, where the 2 Pounder was replaced with a 3" howitzer specifically designed to fit in the same mounting. This did give a very useful HE capability, although 1/3 of the bomb load carried was Smoke ammunition, as the use of this featured highly in British tactical doctrine; such guns were only found in Squadron Headquarters tanks, not within the "sabre" troops.

Yet another disabled Matilda II from France 1940. Notice how the track is sagging away from the suspension units.

The Matilda played a prominent role in the training of new armoured units in the UK from 1940 until around 1943. This CS version is serving with a Valentine unit, as British Valentines did not mount CS weapons and therefore a mix and match policy had to be adopted. Note that the fording markings are different from those shown earlier.

In North Africa the Matilda enjoyed a period of near-invulnerability from the Italian anti-tank guns, but lost it when the Germans arrived in early 1941. In particular, using the 88mm gun in the anti-tank role proved to be decisive in overcoming Matilda's thick frontal armour.

Taken in Tobruk, this Matilda exhibits damage caused by at least three AP hits on the hull, causing the cast section on the side of the hull nose to start to break away along the weld seam.

The tank was also provided with a Vickers (later BESA) coaxial machine gun, and although the authorities would have preferred a second MG to be mounted in the hull front, there was no space. This was because Vulcan had been instructed to design the front of the hull to be similar to the pointed nose of the much-admired Christie medium tank, and this necessitated placing the driver in the centre, prohibiting placing a second crewman alongside him as was standard practice. The turret shell was a casting, and was home to three crewmen – commander, gunner and loader/radio operator. Whilst a three man turret was a sensible decision in that it shared the tasks between the crew and thus allowed the commander more time to actually control the tank, the space allocated was very small and it was a cramped environment to work in for any period of time. All the tanks were designed to take a No 11 (later No 19) wireless set, which further reduced the available space in the turret.

In searching for an engine to power the Matilda II (as it had become known) there was no chance of designing a bespoke powerplant, as Vulcan Foundry was really a locomotive builder and had no experience in internal combustion engines. In order

A Matilda which has changed hands twice, being loaded onto a Scammell tank transporter by a salvage crew in the Western Desert.

to deliver sufficient power for a tank which would weigh over 26 tons (14 tons of which were armour), a novel solution was suggested: use two commercially available engines, and bolt them together to give a doubled power output. (A similarly complicated and difficult to steer solution had been used at the end of WW1 in the Whippet tank.) Initially the engines used were AEC diesels – another novelty for an army wedded to petrol – originally used as a bus engine and each delivering 87 bhp. In order to avoid the steering difficulties experienced with Whippet, the power outputs passed into a common six-speed gearbox. Although the solution generated just about enough power to drive the tank at a maximum speed of about 15 mph, maintenance was difficult. Different engines combinations were used and these, with armament changes, defined the mark designations. In total 5 main versions of the Matilda II were made, as follows.

Another knocked-out Matilda (T6854) in North Africa, with both tracks off thereby immobilising the tank. This version uses the early No 11 radio, with the single thick antenna mounted onto the domed antenna base. Many damaged tanks were recovered and repaired, and the Germans pressed some Matildas into service after recovering them from the battlefield.

The Sunshield deception device was thought up by General Wavell and designed and produced in a very short time in mid-1941, and used extensively in the Western Desert for the next couple of years.

Looking very much like just another lorry – especially from the air – the device was made of painted canvas attached to a lightweight tubular frame. The two soldiers here are sitting on the front of the tank to make it look like a lorry crew, but the real driver had to look out through the dummy radiator.

- A12 Infantry Tank Mk II (Matilda II Mk I) - Vickers coax MG and the AEC 183/184 diesel engines
- A12 Infantry Tank Mk IIA (Matilda II Mk II) - BESA coax MG replaced the Vickers
- A12 Infantry Tank Mk IIA* (Matilda II Mk III) - Leyland 95hp 148/149 or 164/165 diesel engines
- A12 Infantry Tank Mk II (Matilda Mk IV) – improved (rigid) engine mounting for Leyland 170/171, larger fuel capacity
- A12 Infantry Tank Mk II (Matilda Mk V) – as Mk IV but with Westinghouse air servo

Tanks fitted with the 3” howitzer had the letters CS added at the end of the designation.

If the reader finds these confusing then he or she is not alone – the strange nomenclature was the result of a number of different systems in use at the same time. The easiest way is to refer to the four types of Infantry tanks by their names (Matilda I, Matilda II, Valentine, and Churchill) and then by their Mark if appropriate. However, when referring to original documents, it is often necessary to “decode” the terminology, and even during the war, users often got it wrong!

Demonstrating how the device was quickly able to be mounted or discarded, in action a simple release lever would cause the two halves to rotate sideways and then drop off the tank, ready to be collected for re-use later.

Around 9 of the sunshield kits could be stored in one 3 Ton lorry, so two lorries could carry enough Sunshields for an entire squadron of tanks. Note the name of the tank is DANGEROUS, telling us it is a 4RTR tank – they had arrived in Egypt in early 1941 and this tank, T6947, belonged to them.

One side up and the other down showing the tubular framework – the side brackets were permanent fitting on the tank, and were designed to ensure that the frames separated cleanly from the tank, in order to prevent them being damaged as they dropped.

As the tanks still left distinctive tread patterns in the sand from their tracks, brackets were welded on the rear to drag short sections of old track across the track marks, making them look more like the patterns left by the rubber tyres of a real lorry. This so-called "Smoother" device is shown behind a Valentine tank.

Qty	Registrations (military)	Mk	Maker	Remarks
140	T6729 – T6868	II & IIA*	Vulcan	IIA* from T6784. Majority of first 40 to BEF, majority of remainder to North Africa
40	T6869 – T6908	III	Vulcan	Majority of first 20 to North Africa, majority of remainder to USSR
121	T6909 – T7029	II & IIA*	LMSR	IIA* from T6939. Majority to UK or North Africa
80	T7271 – T7350	II & IIA*	Ruston	IIA* from T7291
40	T7351 – T7390	IIA	Ruston	
50	T7391 – T7440	II & IIA*	NBL	IIA* from T7411. Majority to UK or North Africa
40	T10034 – T10073	II & IIA*	Fowler	IIA* from T10060. Majority to UK and North Africa, some to Australia
130	T10074 – T10203	IIA	H&W	IIA* from T10084. Majority to UK and North Africa, some to Australia
80	T10204 – T10283	III & IV	Fowler	Including Scorpion & Baron?
10	T10284 – T10293	I	Vulcan	Mild Steel Instructional, aka A12M
10	T10294 – T10303	IV	Fowler	Majority to North Africa, Australia and USSR
5	T10304 – T10308	III	Ruston	Majority to North Africa, Australia and USSR
5	T10309 – T10313	III	Ruston	To USSR?
50	T10422 – T10471	III	NBL	Majority to NA
100	T17685 – T17784	III & IV	NBL	Majority to USSR and Australia
125	T18761 – T18885	III & IV	Ruston	All to USSR?
100	T18886 – T18985	III & IIICS	LMSR	Majority to North Africa & USSR
95	T18986 – T19080	IV	LMSR	Majority to Australia?
150	T27721 – T27870	IV	Ruston	Majority to USSR and Australia
70	T27871 – T27940	III & IV	H&W	All to USSR
180	T29791 – T29970	IIICS, IVCS & Baron	Vulcan	Some to UK and North Africa, majority of second half of contract to USSR
130	T35148 – T35277	III & IV	NBL	Majority to USSR, a few to Australia
100	T35278 – T35377	III & IV	NBL	To Australia and USSR, a few to UK
110	T37121 – T37230	III & IVCS	LMSR	To UK, Australia and USSR
70	T45964 – T46033	IV	Fowler	All to USSR
75	T46034 – T46108	IV	Fowler	Majority to USSR, a few to Australia
50	T72704 – T72753	IV & IVCS	Vulcan	To North Africa and Australia
200	T72754 – T72953	V	Vulcan	To North Africa, Australia and USSR
75	T82088 – T82162	IV	H&W	First half or so to USSR, remainder to Australia
180	T88064 – T88243	IV & V	Fowler	To USSR and Australia
184	T88244 – T88427	V & Baron	NBL	To USSR and Australia
75	T130770 – T130844	V & Baron	Fowler	Some to Australia and USSR
50	T131126 – T131175	V	Fowler	To Australia and USSR

Another North African Matilda II, painted in the Caunter three-colour camouflage adopted in late 1940; it also sports the White-Red-White recognition markings used from November 1941 onwards and a Tank brigade "diablo" symbol on the turret. The soldier appears to be an Australian guest complete with slouch hat, and is not a member of the tank crew!

A Matilda II captured in North Africa and turned against its former owners – this was common practice by the Afrika Korps who ended up using many more British soft skin vehicles than German ones! This particular tank is noticeably pale, possibly the British Light Stone colour but more likely a German re-paint to remove the original markings, and has been re-marked with large black and white Balkankreuz.

A Russian-operated Matilda c1942, having been knocked out and abandoned, and subsequently captured by the Germans, who then used some of them as the basis for improvised gun carriers. This particular tank arrived in the USSR on 20th March 1942 and was assigned to 183 Tank Brigade.

The tanks saw limited use in France in 1940, with 4RTR possibly having a solitary example for their Commanding Officer, and 7RTR used 27 of them. They acquitted themselves well, taking part in the Arras counter-attack, and their 2 Pounder guns confirmed their reputation as the finest anti-tank gun of the day. In order to improve their mobility by increasing the ground clearance, tanks serving with the BEF had their suspension units raised by around 6", but as this put extra strain on the springs it was not widely adopted elsewhere. Additionally, as the tail-heavy Matilda II tended to drop its rear into trenches when attempting crossings, an extended tail section was added to help prevent this. Although all the BEF Matilda IIs were lost, they started to gain a reputation for being difficult to penetrate by the standard German 37mm anti-tank gun, which to a large degree offset the indifferent mechanical reliability that they exhibited.

The next place that the Matilda II saw action was in North Africa. When the British army went onto the offensive by attacking the Italian forces in Libya, the tank earned the nickname "Queen of the Battlefield" as its maximum 78mm of frontal armour (this

This poor quality shot was probably taken in action – as opposed to being staged – and is probably one of the hundreds of Matilda IIs sent to the USSR from late 1941. Although the armour was appreciated the Russians disliked the insignificant 2 Pounder gun and its inability to fire an HE shell.

1st Armoured Regiment fitters conducting engine maintenance in Borneo, July 1945.

An Australia tank commander adjusting his radio communication equipment; the No 19 radio set was a vast improvement over previous models, and provided the commander with two different frequencies that could be used at the same time on two different radio nets.

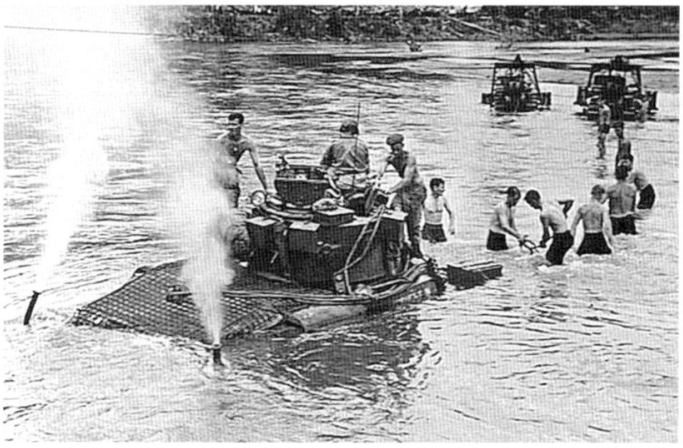

The importance of knowing the fording height! An Australian Matilda crosses a deep river, with the exhaust extensions and anti-grenade mesh screen clearly visible.

Training in combined arms operations in New Guinea. The white markings are the result of the censor, and cover up the tactical markings used.

New Guinea January 1944: Australian crew members maintain a radio watch whilst being ferried ashore. Note the improvised stowage around the rear of the turret.

The armoured louvres have been hinged forwards to allow the crew from 1st Armoured Regiment to conduct daily maintenance and checks, known as "First parade".

was found at the very point of the hull nose plate, there was 75mm on the drivers vertical plate and the turret) made it impervious to Italian anti-tank gunners, and it's still excellent 2 Pounder was easily able to deal with the thinly armoured Italian light and medium tanks. However, with the arrival of the Afrika Korps in February 1941 the Matilda's days were numbered. The new German 50mm anti-tank gun was much more likely to penetrate the armour, and with the introduction of the long 75mm and of

New Guinea, September 1943. Matildas disembark from landing craft in order to provide fire support for Australian infantry.

This CS tank has had a wooden plank fitted across the front of the driver's plate, used to keep stowage items in position and possibly to help protect the driver himself.

Australia received a number of CS Matildas without their 3" gins from New Zealand, and converted them to Frog flamethrower tanks, a very useful weapon in clearing Japanese bunkers. It was NOT advisable for infantryman to sit on the tank when it was in action!

Matildas of the 2/9th Armoured Regiment awaiting overhaul at Wondecla in Queensland after the end of a divisional exercise. They still have the fording height markings (useful in jungle terrain) and have had Australia-specific modifications made to them; most have had the 4" smoke bomb throwers removed.

The original engine used on the Matilda was the AEC diesel 183/184, actually two 87 bhp engines bolted together and used to drive a common transmission. This is the engine from the front...

...and here it is from the right side.

course the use of the 88mm anti-aircraft gun in the anti-tank role, the advantage bestowed by the Matilda's armour was negated, and in all other respects the tank had passed its use by date against a first-class enemy. In a similar way to the Matilda I, it was often used in a quasi-Cruiser role, not supporting infantry directly in the way it was designed for but operating in a more mobile and free-ranging style, although its slow speed did not really suit that. However, the inability of the design to be up-gunned and mount the 6 Pounder doomed it to obsolescence. Again, memoirs of soldiers who fought in the tank during the desert campaign can provide us with interesting insights into the tank, its capabilities, and the type of warfare it was used in:

On the Mk III the Leyland 148/149 was used, giving another 16 bhp of power. This is the front of that engine.

This is the left rear view of the Leyland 148/149. The 164/165 version also used on the Mk III was similar.

During this attack he took on a battery of 105mm guns, one of which scored a hit on his cupola, blowing in the episcope, wounding him and killing his gunner. In spite of further track damage, he was able to withdraw to the rally point... The appearance of the Matildas proved decisive, and by 1700 hours all fighting in Bardia had ceased...The Australians were delighted with the support they received from 7RTR, and Waltzing Matilda took on a new meaning...Although 7RTR had managed to get 8 tanks as far as Mechili, the battle was now going too fast for them...The Italians were learning. As the Matildas reared up over the walls and other obstacles, the artillerymen chose their aiming-points on the vehicles thin belly plates, and scored seven kills...The inability to fire an HE round proved fatal...the Mark II does not even shake itself when the first shots go ricocheting off its thick hide...

When the Germans invaded the USSR in June 1941 the Russians had developed an excellent tank, the T34, but there were not enough of them and Stalin requested urgent help from Britain. Churchill was only too anxious to strike the Nazis wherever he could, and he saw the supply of equipment to the Soviet regime as a way of doing this. He therefore ordered that military equipment of all types, including tanks, were to be shipped to

The Mk IV used a rigid engine mounting for the Leyland 170/171 engine, plus had a larger fuel capacity. This is the front...

the USSR, starting the infamous arctic convoy system. When they received the Matildas, starting at the end of 1941, the crews appreciated the armour but thought of the 2 Pounder as ineffective, which by that stage it was, coming up against the up-armoured German tanks. The Soviets preferred the 3" howitzer armed CS versions, although they were not really interested in the smoke round and constantly pressed for more HE ammunition. Around 1000 were shipped, although around 1/4 were lost on route. The tank was nothing more than a stop-gap, but it did help to stabilise the situation in Russia, gaining time for

...and this is the rear.

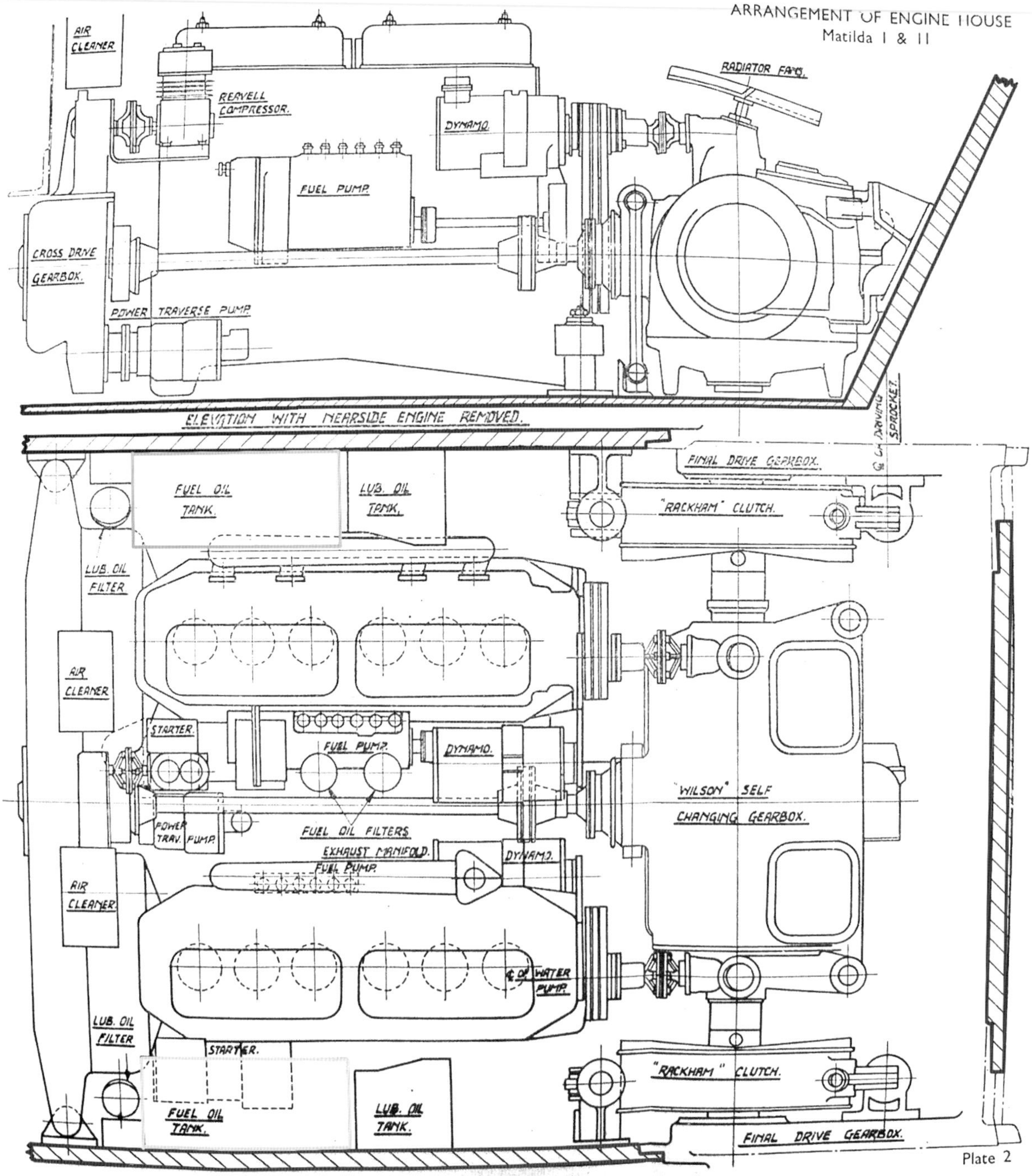

Taking from an official workshop manual, this diagram shows how the engine was laid out on Mk I and II vehicles, from the side with the nearest engine not shown (top), and from above (underneath. It also shows the main engine components.

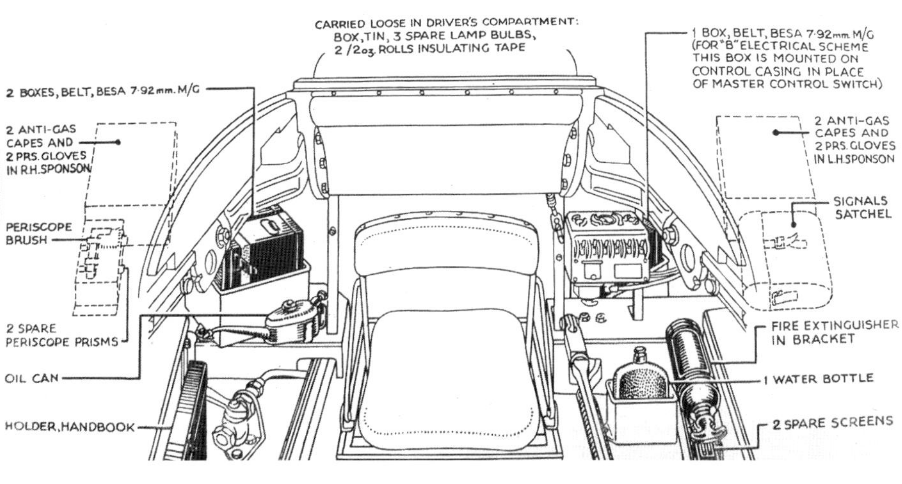

The driver's compartment layout varied slightly between the different marks, but this shows the basic layout, as if looking into the cab from outside, with the driver's visor fully opened. Every spare inch of volume was used for stowage.

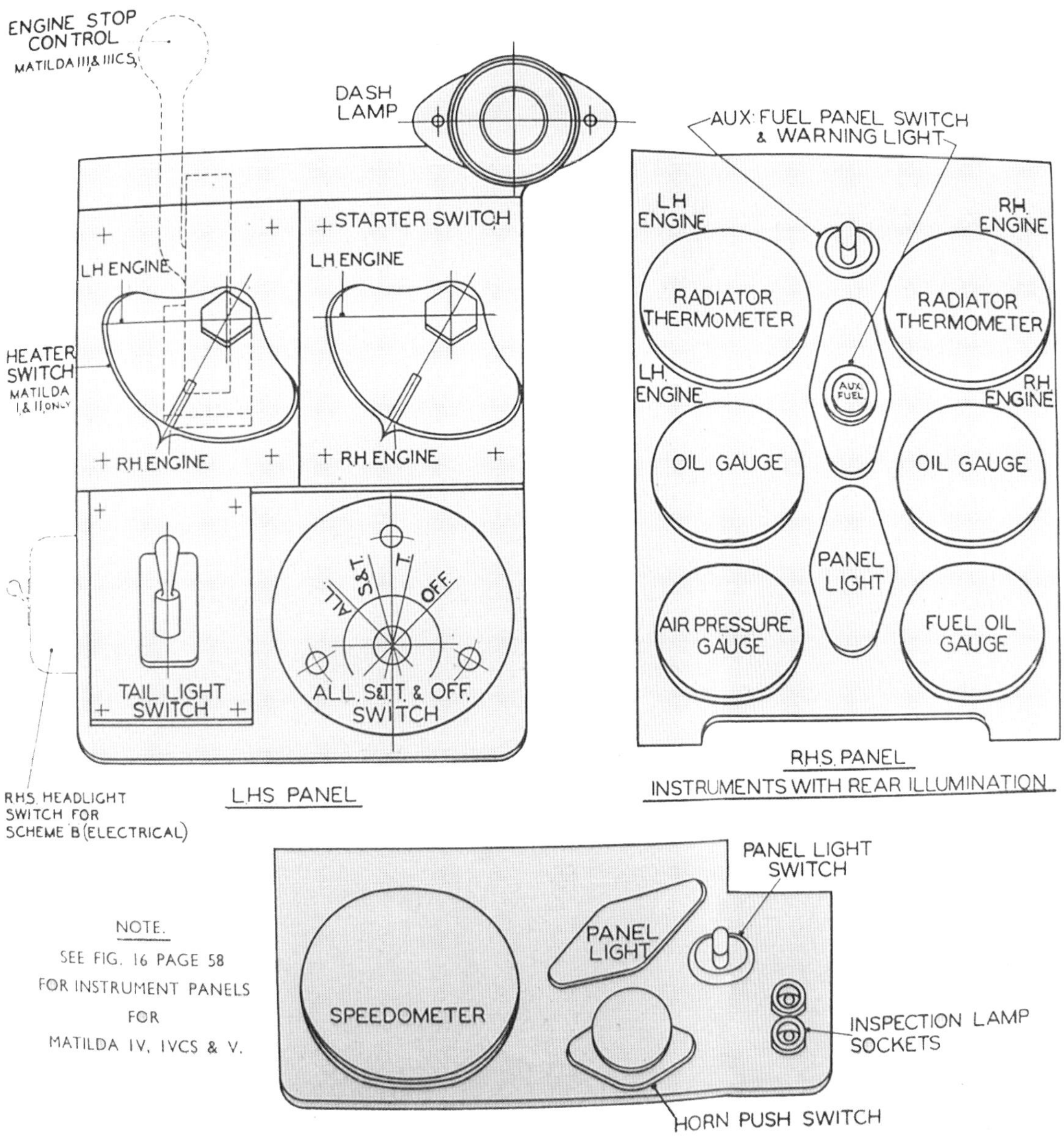

The main driver's instrument panel was mounted to his front right, and needed to contain the instruments for both engines separately. The speedometer was mounted separately to his left.

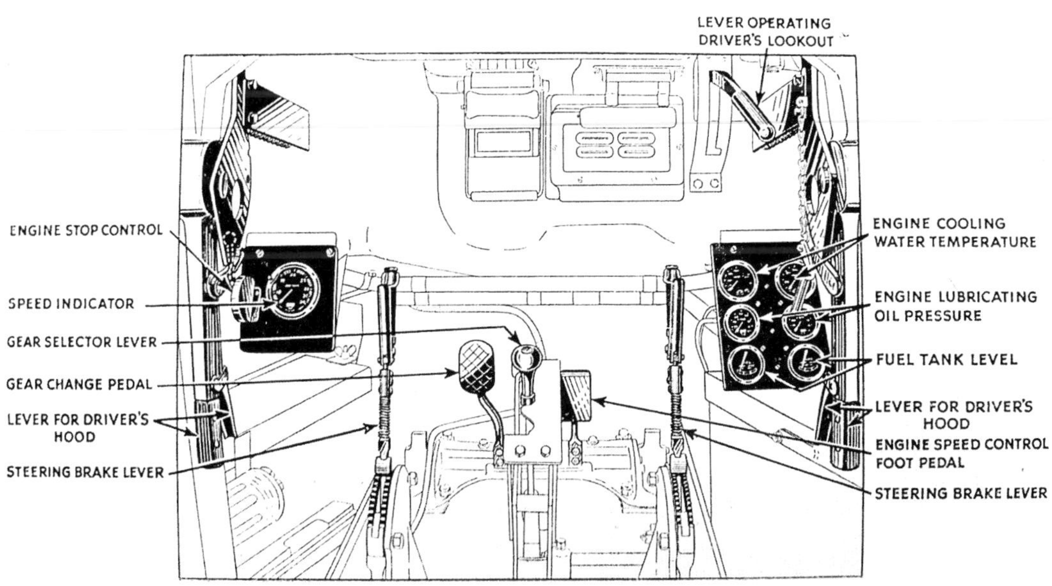

The driver's view of his controls; braking was achieved not with a foot pedal but by pulling both steering levers (the "sticks") back together. They could be locked in the rear position and used as a handbrake function by operating the spring-loaded levers at the top of each stick.

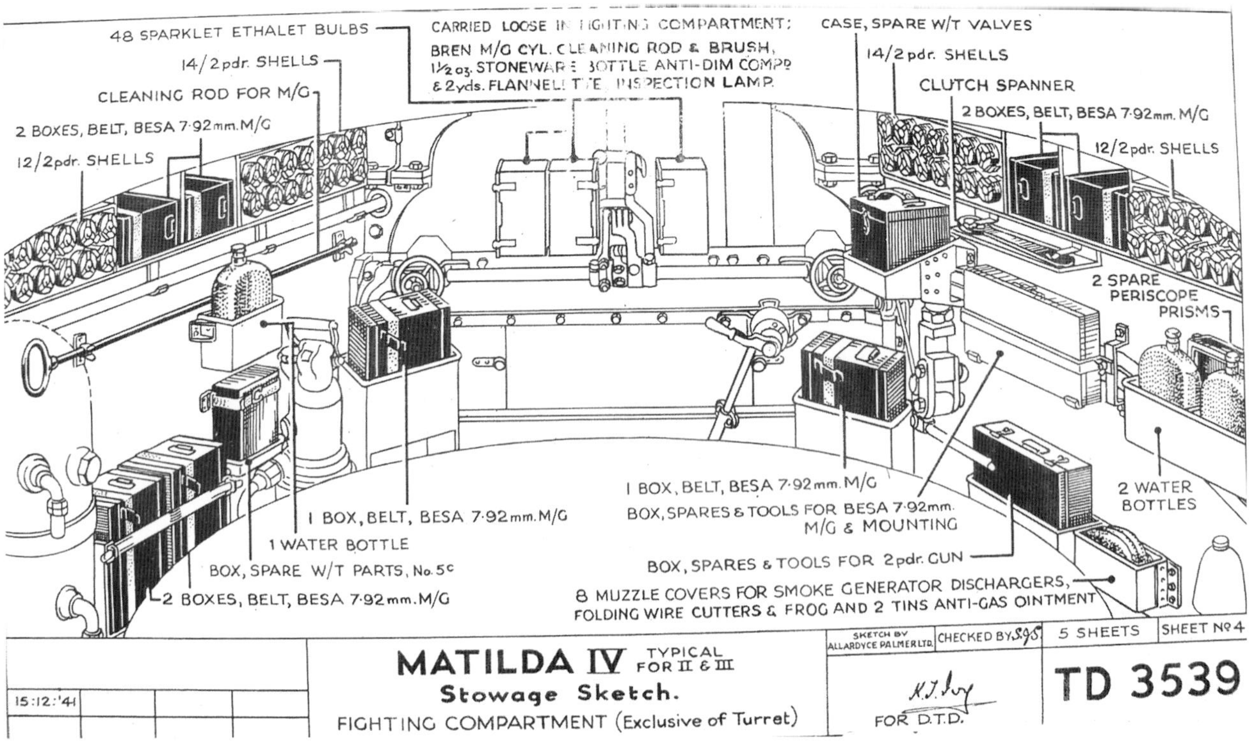

Stowage in the fighting compartment again varied between marks, and the ammunition layout for the CS versions had to accommodate the larger 3" ammunition, and the early Vickers-armed versions also had MG ammunition stowage to suit that gun. This diagram shows the Mk IV, but the II, III and V were all similar

the USSR to produce the T34 in increasing quantities until the Matilda was no longer useful in front-line service.

The other recipient for large numbers of Matildas, even when it had become obsolete in Europe, was Australia. The newly-formed Australian Armoured Corps found that the tank was a useful weapon for the types of terrain it was fighting in during the Pacific campaign, and its armour again proved useful, giving adequate protection against the smaller calibre Japanese guns. Britain supplied over 400 Matildas to Australia, along with 33 CS tanks from New Zealand of which 18 had the guns removed for mounting in Valentines (see below). The Australians modified the tanks to suit the conditions they

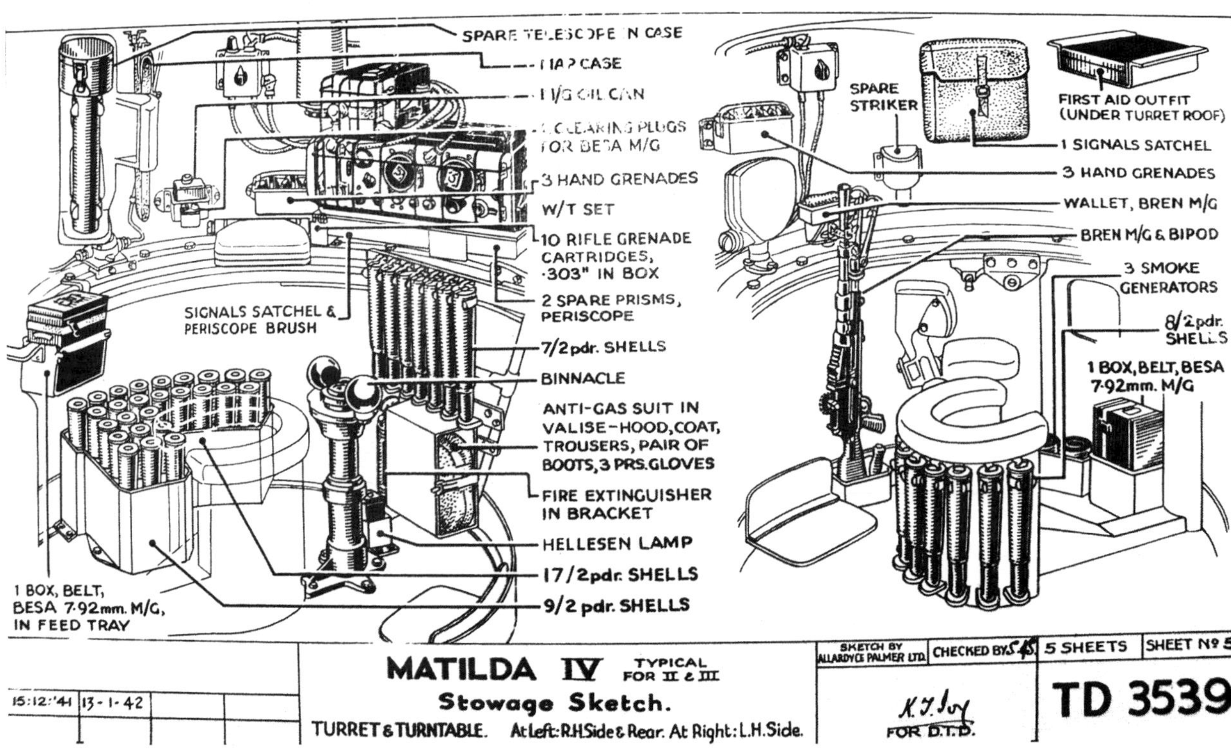

The Mk IV again, showing just how crowded the inside of the turret was when fully stowed with tools and ammunition – as well as three crewmen! 41 of the two pounder shells were stowed as "ready rounds", allowing a fast rate of fire.

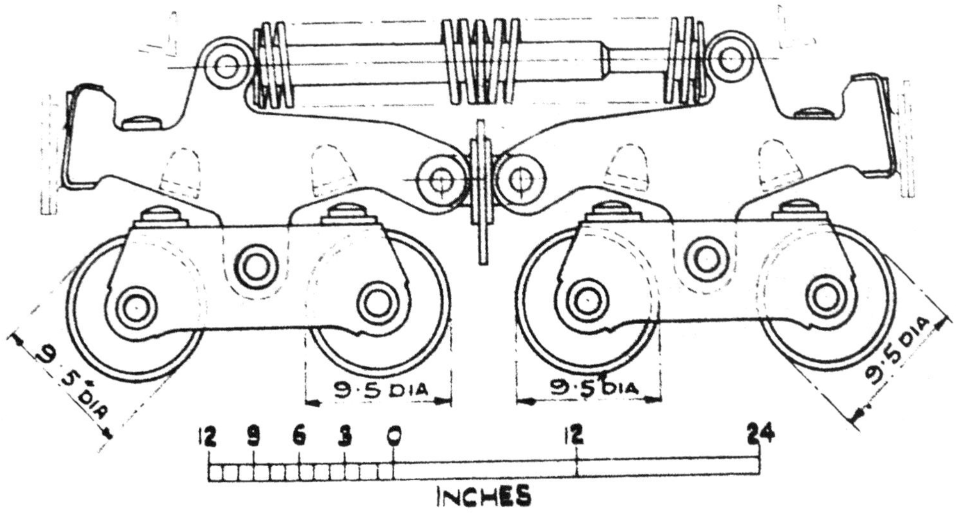

The complicated suspension of the Matilda was difficult to get to for servicing and maintenance, as it was hidden behind the armoured mud chutes. This image shows how the central pairs of small roadwheels pivoted together against a common shock absorbing spring.

T35357 was made by North British Locomotives and was converted in Australia to a Hedgehog:

Some Australian Matildas had these 1 7/8" cast steel front mudguards fitted in place of the usual stiff rubber types, and were designed to protect the idler wheel and track adjusting gear from damage.

BESA firing: attacking Japanese positions on Tarakan island in July 1945. The unit is 2/9th Australian Armoured Regiment.

Loading the canister into one of the 4" smoke bomb throwers mounted on the right side of the turret.

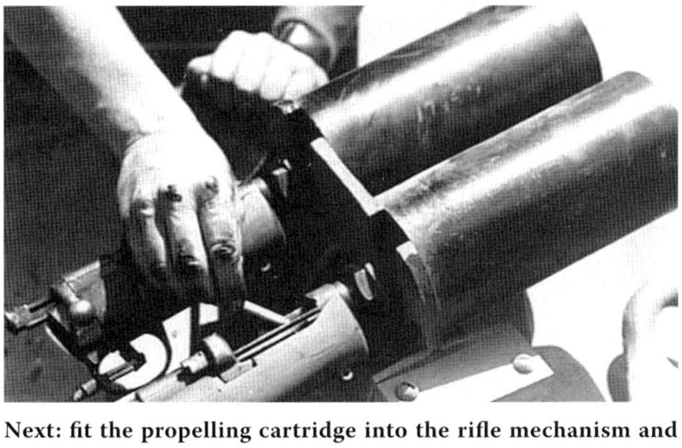

Next: fit the propelling cartridge into the rifle mechanism and close the bolt.

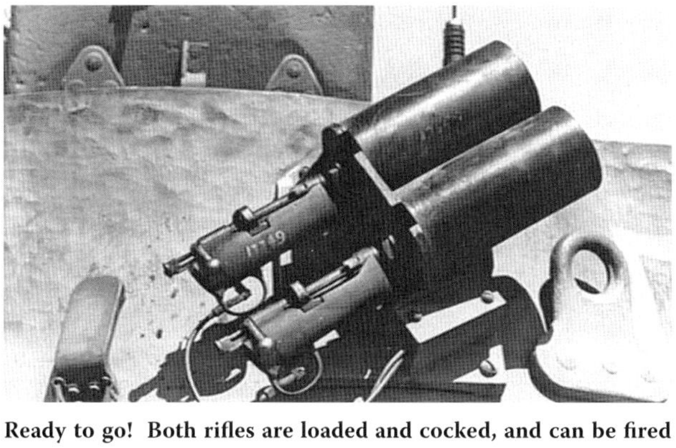

Ready to go! Both rifles are loaded and cocked, and can be fired by operating a cable from inside the turret.

4th Armoured Brigade training in Queensland Australia, and showing off the tactical markings used. The 25 symbol is the Matilda's bridge classification, roughly equivalent to its weight in tons.

Queen of the Desert! The classic image of the Matilda at the height of its powers, speeding (OK, moving) across the desert in 1941.

would be used in, including adding extra protection against grenade and sticky bomb attack. They also rebuilt some of the New Zealand-supplied Matildas as flamethrowers, known as Frogs, and fitted others with batteries of rocket projectiles on the hull rear; these were known as Hedgehogs. It was with the Australian forces that the Matilda was still involved in active operations at the end of the war, tribute indeed to an unlikely tank made by a locomotive builder who could only provide two inexperienced designers for the tank!

Infantry Tank Mk III Valentine

The third infantry tank adopted by the British was never given an A series designation, as it came about as the result of a private venture proposal by Vickers-Armstrong, which was initially rejected by the army until the pressing need for any sort of tanks led to it entering service in April 1940, too late for any to serve during the campaign in France in 1940. Eventually over 7000 were produced, not only in Britain but also in Canada, where 1420 Valentines were made by the Canadian Pacific Railroad company in Montreal, the majority being shipped to the USSR. In a similar way to the Matilda II, the need to find other companies to build the Valentine eventually led to Metro-Cammell and the Birmingham Railway Carriage Company producing tanks to the Vickers design.

Although the tank was in many ways an indifferent design, it possessed certain attributes that meant it remained in use until the end of the war. In part this was due to a number of specialised variants that were made using the chassis, most notably the Scissors Bridgelayer and the Archer self-propelled gun, as well as Duplex Drive swimming variants. However, it was also due to the inherent simplicity of the design which allowed it to be re-engined and up-gunned throughout its life. The designer, Sir John Carden, was totally adamant that the tank must remain

A new Mk II or IV Valentine on the back of a lorry and apparently destined for the USSR; many British workers had Soviet sympathies during the war and sending any sort of military aid to the Russians was one of Churchill's methods of taking the fight to Germany.

A Polish Valentine used as the subject of, and the platform for, a series of still and movie films, although why the camera crew feel the need to wear steel helmets is unknown!

The tank is either a Mk II or IV – externally they were identical, the difference being in the type of engine, AEC in the Mk II, GMC in the Mk IV.

within its original weight limit; otherwise its power-to-weight ratio would reduce as would its mobility. He (and subsequently others) successfully resisted weight increases, even managing to up-gun the tank twice without reducing its agility (and which is why Valentines were never fitted with armoured mud-chutes over the suspension). It only had a crew of three, at a time when most tanks required five men; this was an advantage to the army when trying to train large numbers of men to crew its expanding armoured forces, but a disadvantage in battle, as there were less men to carry out all the necessary maintenance, and two man

The turret has been reversed for this shot, which affords us great views of the "slow-motion" suspension units and the side stowage bins.

The background for the series seems to be on a bomb-damaged airfield, maybe to give the product an air of authenticity – although the tank commander looks bored with the whole affair!

A great close-up of the hull and turret details. Both driver's hatches are open; the driver had two hatches which allowed him a better chance of escape if one was blocked by the position of the gun barrel.

A Valentine unit, with a Matilda CS in support, is overflown by a Westland Lysander army cooperation aircraft on an exercise in UK. These were frequently used to drop messages to troops in the field on exercises, but there are no indications that they were ever used in action in this way. The cross on the tank front denotes "enemy".

turrets always overwork the commander. The Valentine was also small and inconspicuous which made it a difficult target to hit, it was relatively well armoured particularly from the frontal aspect, and was also generally reliable. Initially armed with the same 2 Pounder as used on the Matilda II, the Valentine possessed the virtue that it could be up-gunned and improved. The Mk I, II and IV 2 Pounder variants were superseded with the Mk III and V which featured a three man turret to replace the inefficient two man version used on the early marks. This was really a case of pouring a quart into a pint pot: the turret was only marginally larger, and the commander sat just out of the path of the recoiling gun at the rear of the turret! The next version, the Mark IX was armed with the much more effective 6 Pounder, as was the Mk X; the Mk IX was however handicapped by a frankly crazy decision not to mount a coaxial MG in the turret, which made it extremely unpopular, and which was rectified on the Mk X. As the 6 Pounder could be easily modified to increase its calibre from 57mm to 75mm, the final mark, the Mk XI used that weapon which came with the bonus that it could fire a useful HE shell.

The Mk I version was powered by a 135 bhp petrol AEC 189 engine, but all subsequent marks used diesel engines. The AEC 190, a 131 bhp compression-ignition engine was used in the Mk II and III, and an American designed GMC 6004 developing 138 bhp was used in the Mk IV, V, VI, VII and IX (there was no Mk VIII). The GMC engine was then uprated to 165 bhp, and used in late models of the Mk IX, as well as the Mk X and XI. The new engines did not make it notably faster; it was always a relatively slow tank with a maximum speed of only about 15mph, the same as the Matilda II. However, unlike the Matilda, the Valentine could keep going at that speed all day long, even when tackling gradients that caused the Matilda to slow down significantly. The diesel engines added reliability and increased range, and were simple to maintain.

Production by the four companies involved totalled 7315 tanks, broken down as 5562 x 2 Pounder-armed (including 160 DDs), 1458 x 6 Pounder-armed (including 312 DDs), and 295 x 75mm-armed (including 175 DDs). In addition, 217 Bridgelayers, 101 Bishop 25 Pounder SPG and 667 Archer 17 Pounder SPG were built on the chassis.

Registrations	Quantity and mark	Maker
T15946 - T16220	175 x I (to 16120) 100 x II (from 18121)	Vickers Armstrong
T16221 - T16345	44 x I 81 x II	Metropolitan Cammell
T16356 – T16355	67 x I (to 16421) 133 x II (from 16422)	Birmingham Railway Carriage Co
T17360 – T17384	25 x II	Birmingham Railway Carriage Co
T17385 – T17684	299 x II	Birmingham Railway Carriage Co
T18071 – T18095	25 x II	Metropolitan Cammell
T20419 – T20493	22 x I (to 20440) 53 x II (from 20441)	Metropolitan Cammell
T23204 - T23503	300 x VI/VII	Canadian Pacific Railroad
T27121 - T27420	250 x II 50 x IV	Vickers Armstrong
T27421 – T27720	214 x II 85 or 86 x IV	Metropolitan Cammell
T32471 - T32720	81 x II (T32531-T32595, T32685-T32720 (inc 20x B/L) 149 x IV (T32471-T32530, T32596-T32684)	Metropolitan Cammell
T32721 – T32970	210 x II	Birmingham Railway Carriage Co
T40981 - T41430	450 x VI/VII	Canadian Pacific Railroad
T47098 – T47347	250 x IV	Vickers Armstrong
T66466 – T66590	125 x IV	Vickers Armstrong
T66591 – T67220	230 x IX	Vickers Armstrong
T67221 – T67260	40 x IV	Metropolitan Cammell
T67261 – T67865	545 x V (T67321-T67865) inc 85 x DD (non-sequential) plus 60 bridgelayer hulls (T67261-T67320).	Metropolitan Cammell
T73554 - T74193	640 x VI/VII	Canadian Pacific Railroad
T82163 – T82617	75 x VDD 16 x IX 312 x IXDD	Metropolitan Cammell
T120690 – T120949	30 x IX 35 x X 20 x XI 175 x XIDD	Metropolitan Cammell
T122698 – T123157	460 x IX	Vickers Armstrong
T123158 – T123632	275 x IX 100 x X 100 x XI	Vickers Armstrong
CT138916 - CT138945	30 x VI/VII	Canadian Pacific Railroad

A rare colour image showing a Soviet Valentine being lifted by a crane, the lifting tackle being attached to the lifting eyes fitted front and rear. Note the track and suspension sag in the middle.

In a spot of bother! This tank belonging to 11th Armoured Division appears to have come off the road, or possibly broken down, in a very inconvenient location. Note the damage to the front mudguards.

Stand back children! FROBISHER belonging to a unit of 8th Armoured Division, probably C Sqn of 46RTR. The unit shipped out to the Middle East in July 1942, this photograph is believed to be dated to 1941.

Another tank in a bigger spot of bother! From the position of the other two tanks, it appears that they are about to attempt some troop recovery, dragging the drowned tank rearwards out of the swamp.

At only around 16 tons the Valentine was small and light enough to be lifted easily, and carried either on train flats or on the flatbed of a truck, no specialist tank transporter being necessary.

Unloading in Egypt, MOHAWK belonged to C Sqn 40RTR, who arrived in North Africa in July 1942 as part of 23rd Armoured Brigade. This brigade used Valentines in lieu of the cruiser tanks that it should have been equipped with, and performed extremely well.

The censor has attacked the markings on the front of this Valentine in North Africa. Despite its many good qualities, by 1942 the Valentine was past its "use by" date, and the two-man turret was an anachronism which handicapped efficient use of the tank in action.

The Valentine proved fairly popular in Russian service, although these examples have been captured by the Germans during winter operations. Note that the soldiers are dragging sleds behind them, probably used for extracting casualties.

As the Valentine was ordered into production too late to see service in 1940, it made its battlefield debut in North Africa with 8RTR during Operation CRUSADER in November 1941. Again, it is worth noting that in a similar way to both models of the Matilda but even moreso, the Valentine was often used in the Cruiser role. In large part this was because Britain had concentrated her efforts from 1940 onwards into building I-tanks rather than Cruisers, which led to an imbalance in numbers when the open spaces of the Egyptian and Libyan deserts required Cruiser tanks. Indeed, during 1942 Valentine-equipped units (variously 8, 40, 46 and 50RTR at different times) formed the order of battle

A Valentine crewman poses by his tank in a rear area (note the tents, not used in the front line areas). Many Valentine crewmen seemed to have had developed a real affection for the tank, despite its many shortcomings as a weapon of war.

Knocked out Valentines in North Africa: despite its reasonable armour, many tanks were lost due to faulty tactical use, including the attack on Ruweisat ridge in July 1942, when the newly-arrived 23rd Armoured Brigade got itself into fatal trouble in a large minefield. Note the damage to the muzzle of the 2 Pounder.

Afrika Korps soldiers investigate knocked-out or broken down Valentines. T32722 was a Mk II made by the Birmingham Railway Carriage Company, one of the firms brought in to make the Vickers-designed tanks.

of 23rd Armoured Brigade, which should have been equipped with Cruisers but which used Valentines instead. By the end of the North African campaign in May 1943 the Valentine had earned a reputation as a reliable but never spectacular tank, with good armour and the ability to maintain consistent speed largely untroubled by gradients and terrain. It was clearly obsolete in its current form, even though the first few 6 Pounder examples had been issued, and by 1943 most units operating it were re-equipped with either more modern I-Tanks (Churchills) or true Cruisers (Shermans). During the campaign Bishop self-propelled

ALI BABA is either a Mk III or V, featuring the 2 Pounder armed three man turret brought into service in an attempt to improve the fightability and ergonomics of the Valentine. This tank possibly belonged to 17th/21st Lancers, who fought in Tunisia in 1943.

Valentines and Matildas on the way to the USSR; although some of the tanks sent were brand new, particularly from 1943 onwards, many were taken directly from army units in the UK.

guns were also used, as well as a number of Valentines converted into Scorpion mine-clearing flail tanks. It must also be noted that the Valentine performed a valuable role in the UK from 1941 to 1943, equipping new armoured units and formations with a reliable - there is that word again – tank which allowed them to gain experience and to practice manouevre without worrying unduly about excessive breakdowns.

The story might have largely ended there was it not for the invention of the Duplex Drive swimming tank by Nicholas Straussler. Initially testing the concept using the Tetrarch light

Another Valentine being investigated by German soldiers in North Africa – as well as assessing its salvage potential, they may just be looking for food and cigarettes!

German soldiers, some wearing Zeltbahn capes, investigating a Soviet Valentine Mk II or IV. The transmission decks are both up which may indicate a breakdown, but there is at least one AP shot hole visible.

The trackguards on Valentines were fairly flimsy, and many photographs show that they were badly knocked about in combat conditions. This photograph has all the hallmarks of a captured tank being used for the WW2 equivalent of a "selfie"!

A posed photograph showing Red army tank riders perched on a Valentine. Although a very small tank, there are still no less than ten infantrymen armed with PPSH SMGs on the tank!

John Pearson's magnificently restored Valentine Mk IXDD, restored over twenty years after being found in a number of pieces, including the turret which had been cut up.

The rear of John's DD, taken on the beach, although the tank is too unique to attempt swimming! The canvas of the screen is in an authentic colour known as Mountbatten Pink.

The rear of this wartime DD shows the single propeller at the rear underneath the folded screen. DDs were converted from specially constructed watertight hulls, and were invaluable in training crews for the Normandy landings.

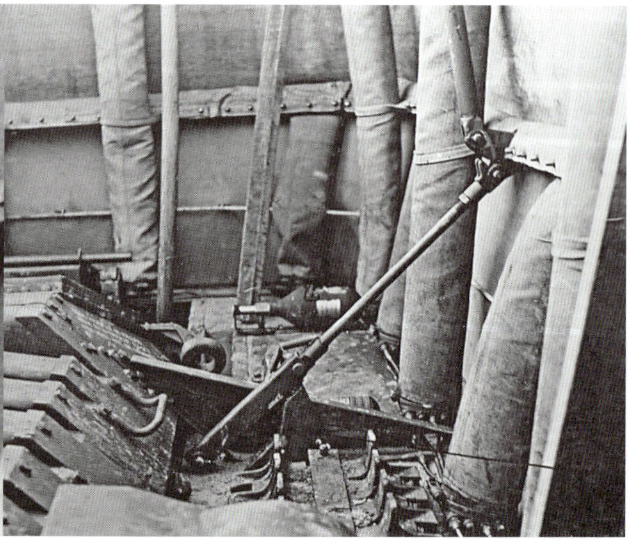

Two images showing inside the DD with the screens erected. They were inflated using compressed air which filled the tubular pillars, and then locked in place with knuckled metal rods.

This image shows one of the prototype DDs with the screen folded and the steering periscope raised on the turret roof. The modification to the shape of the front hull can be clearly seen.

tank, it was decided to build substantial numbers of Valentine DD models to train and equip the armoured units selected to swim ashore in the invasion of Europe. Trials began in mid-1942, and orders for hundreds of the tanks soon followed. The tanks were not built as DDs, but were converted into the configuration subsequently. Both 2 Pounder and 6 Pounder armed models were turned into DDs, despite the realisation that the performance of the latter would marginal by 1944, and the former was totally obsolete on a gun tank, and should be used only on armoured cars. It was sensibly decided to develop the DD concept for use on Sherman tanks armed with 75mm guns, but production difficulties led to them being produced much slower than anticipated, and the last of the Valentine DDs were only replaced a few days before D-Day! They also saw some active service in Italy, with 7th Hussars operating DD Valentines at the end of hostilities there.

These walkaround shots show the Virginia Museum's restored Mk III (Courtesy Scott Taylor). The slightly longer turret used to accommodate a third crewman can be seen, but the tank still only mounted the (by then) outclassed 2 Pounder.

The front of the hull left hand side, showing one of the pair of driver's hatches open, and the exhaust pipe fishtail.

The small circular hatch on the side of the turret was often used to discard used cartridge cases out of the tank, although officially it was a pistol post, used to defend the tank against infantry at close range!

However, Valentines did see other operational service in other theatres up to the very end of the war. In the Far East 50th Indian Tank Brigade used them until July 1944, and Valentine Mks IX, X and XI were used by artillery regiments supporting infantry divisions in the liberation of North West Europe 1944 – 45. Between three and four thousand British and Canadian-built Valentines were sent to the USSR, although many hundreds were sunk on the way. But sufficient remained for the Soviets to make good use of them, and of all the British, indeed Allied tanks that they received, they seem to have thought quite highly of

The Mk III and Mk V used the same turret, with a distinctive surround to the mantlet that provided a little more armour to the front of the turret. The small hole alongside is the object lens of the gunner's telescopic sight.

The different cast textures of the mantlet surround and the turret side walls are very noticeable. The four bolts on the circular plate are the trunnion caps, the point that the gun elevates and depresses about.

A close up of the armoured "plug" of the pistol post in a slightly opened position – it was operated by a lever inside the turret.

Mounted on the rear of the turret is one of the two antenna bases for the No 19 radio set, here the short range B set, and a stowage box for six 100 round drum magazines for the anti-aircraft Bren MG.

British practice was to stow tools on the trackguards, and most tank's carried a number of spare track links to allow repairs to be carried out in the field.

The two large headlamps were vulnerable to damage in action, and so were often either reversed so that they pointed into the hull, and/or had steel helmets slung over them.

Note that the headlamps are mounted on sprung brackets, to prevent the bulbs breaking due to vibration.

The distinctive sloping rear hull of the Valentine, common to all the marks. The engine is under the front (horizontal) louvres, and the transmission under the sloping pair.

The handles on the sides of the engine louvres were used to lift the decks up and towards the centre – note the top hinges. If necessary, the whole louvre set could be quickly removed to allow better access to engine components.

Underneath the transmission louvres is a stowage box for five Petrol, Oils and Lubricant (POL) cans, although water was often also stowed there. It was important to place the lids at the top, to help prevent leaks.

Alongside the rear trackguard but not fitted would be the rear (red) tail light – the bracket and junction box can be seen.

The external stowage boxes on the track guards were used for stowing specific items of crew kit, including greatcoats and blankets, as well as smaller tools and the crew's rations.

The front left quarter of the tank, demonstrating how far (or not) the driver's hatch could be opened. The ideal Valentine driver was small in stature, as getting in and out, and being comfortable once in was difficult for a larger man.

The right hand side turret rear, with the A set antenna base for the radio set, used for longer range communication, normally to Squadron or Regimental headquarters.

The front right of the turret, with the coaxial BESA MG alongside the 2 Pounder. Note the rough texture to parts of the mantlet surround, and how the front of the turret is bolted to the sides.

Alongside the BESA can be seen a large circular hole – this is the muzzle of a 2" smoke bomb thrower, which replaced the older external 4" version used on Matildas etc.

The turret used an arrangement of three hatches, and the front section mounts a Vickers tank periscope in a rotating mount. This was better than a fixed mount, but nowhere near as good as a proper cupola.

the Valentines. This is probably because it was small, reasonably armoured, simple to maintain and operate, and reliable; in other words, all the traits that endeared it to its British crews. It is likely that Valentines were used by Soviet armoured reconnaissance units up to and including the entry into Berlin, after which they were rapidly retired. Finally, we must note the New Zealand use of the Valentine in the Pacific campaign. Over 250 were sent to New Zealand, where they were used in that country for defence

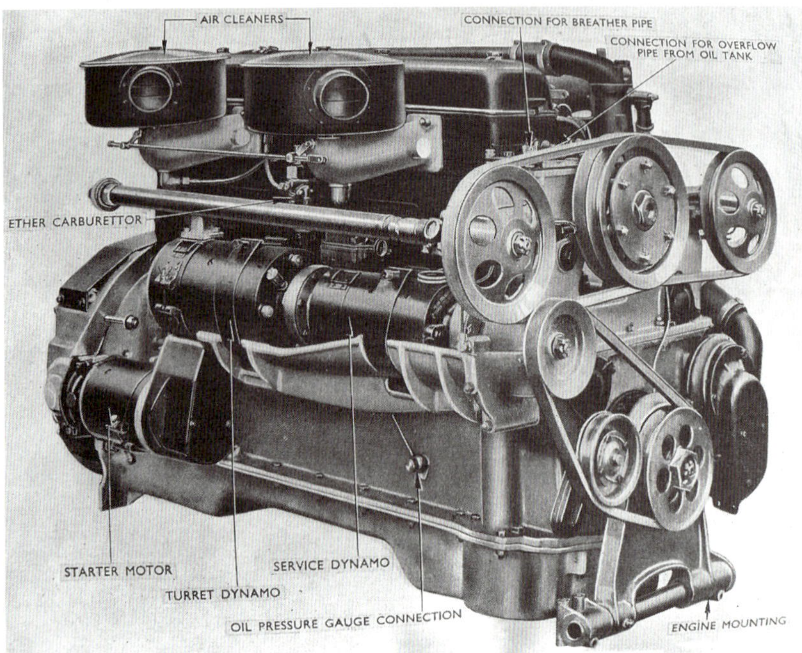

The AEC 190 diesel engine was used on the Mk II and Mk III versions of the Valentine; this is the right hand side.

A surprisingly effective Valentine variant was the Archer self-propelled gun, which used the extremely accurate and hard-hitting 17 pounder. However, the only way of making it fit was to mount if rearwards, over the rear decks!

The venerable Valentine served with the New Zealand armoured corps until the end of the 1950s, and is shown here in service with them (Courtesy Jeffrey Plowman).

and training purposes. 18 Mk IIIs were converted into the close support role by fitting 3" howitzers taken from some of the 33 Matilda II CS tanks supplied to them. This was no mean feat, as the British army did not believe it was possible to do this, and as a result had equipped its Valentine tank regiments with CS Matildas instead! The converted tanks were used in action only once, in support of 3rd NZ Infantry Division in February 1944, where their close support delivering an 18lb HE shell would have been welcomed. They continued in service, in dwindling numbers, in New Zealand until finally being retired in the late 1950s.

Not a true variant, bur definitely a "funny"! A Valentine hull turned into an APC – or possibly a mobile pillbox – in Cyprus during the invasion of 1974.

A drawing of the A20 heavy infantry tank – the basic layout was scaled down to become the A22. Note the Matilda II type turret and the ludicrous side-mounted machine guns, a throwback to the sorts of design used in WW1.

A22 Infantry Tank Mk IV Churchill

It is worth beginning by noting three key facts about the Churchill from the outset. Firstly, it was so horribly unreliable when it was first produced that serious consideration was given to stopping production; in May 1942 the Director of Military Operations, Major General Kennedy, wrote that: "The Churchill cannot be regarded as anything more than a stop-gap, and should be replaced as soon as possible". Secondly, as well as its primary role as a gun tank, it was the basis for many of the essential specialist variants – the Funnies – that enabled D-Day and subsequent operations to be successful. Thirdly, of the four infantry tanks that Britain produced during WW2, it was the only one that was consistently used in the role that it was designed for, the close support of the infantry, and which proved to be successful. Despite its awful debut it went onto to become the best – and final – infantry tank that Britain was to build, as by 1944 it was clear that both the requirement and the technical know-how existed to build tanks that could function as both Cruisers and as I-tanks, and which would come to dominate the battlefield of the future. But in the context of WW2, the Churchill gained a reputation as a tank that could take a hit and allow the crew to stand a good chance of survival; studies conducted during the war indicated that of all the tanks used by the British, Canadian and American crews in France and Italy, the Churchill gave its crews the best percentage chances of escaping unhurt, and that in itself is no bad epithet.

A Mk I Churchill in the hands of a Canadian unit in UK. The utility of the 3" howitzer fitted to the hull was severely restricted by its limited traverse and elevation, which was proved during the Dieppe raid of August 1942. This tank has been refitted with the trackguards and the second style air intakes.

In some tanks, the 2 Pounder and 3" howitzers were switched around, which merely transferred the problems of the hull mounting to the smaller weapon, plus giving problems with the internal ammunition stowage! This tank has the early air intakes and no trackguards.

T68176R BETTY was one of 18 Mk IIIs used in the Dieppe raid in August 1942. She was the tank of the troop sergeant of 7 Tp B Sqn The Calgary Regiment, and carries the deep wading equipment used by the tanks on the raid. The Germans were unimpressed by the appearance and fighting qualities of the Churchill, and concluded that they had only been used in the raid because they could afford to be thrown away!

In the month that Britain declared war on Germany, it was decided to produce a new large infantry tank, known as the A20. Designed and built in prototype form by Harland & Wolff of Belfast, its layout was a throwback to WW1, with sponson mounted guns on the sides as well as in a turret. It was quickly realised that it possessed a number of deficiencies, not least of which was it sheer size, making it difficult to transport around and slow to produce. Therefore, it was decided to initiate another smaller infantry tank design, based in part upon the A20 and called the A22, which would eventually gain lasting fame as the Churchill.

Another of the Dieppe tanks, this is one of the eleven Mk I tanks used. Although many accounts refer to the tanks not being able to leave the beaches due to becoming stuck in the pebbles; this is incorrect: they were restricted to the beaches because the Germans had blocked the roads leading into the town, preventing the tanks from breaking through and restricting them to supporting the exposed infantry on the beaches.

Operation JUBILEE. A general scene showing the unfolding drama at Dieppe, with T68559R CALGARY of C Sqn The Calgary Regiment in the foreground, after the tide had come in and partially submerged some of the vehicles. Although the raid was a disaster, many important lessons were learned that would lead to the success of the D-Day landings in 1944.

The task of designing the A22 was given to Vauxhall Motors, an experienced car manufacturer, under strict instructions to introduce it into service as rapidly as possible; Winston Churchill had demanded 500 of the new tanks within a year. The only way to achieve this was to go straight into production without any prototypes being built, or reliability etc trials being conducted. This would invariably mean that it would enter service with a number of teething troubles, and the risk of this was accepted because of the prevailing war situation. In order to speed things up the basic layout proposed for the A20 was to be re-used on the A22, as was the suspension and track layout, everything being scaled down as necessary. Entering

Seven of the Dieppe tanks towed Daimler Scout Cars ashore – this appears to be Churchill I T31107R BOLSTER towing HELEN.

Probably the most famous photograph of the Dieppe raid, with a Churchill III from 9 Troop B Sqn. These tanks were named in very un-warlike fashion BUTTERCUP, BLOSSOM and BLUEBELL.

service in June 1941 only 12 months after its specification was still being confirmed, it became immediately apparent that to call the tank's problems teething troubles was an understatement of massive proportions. The user handbook was prefaced with as close to an apology as one could ever see in an official publication, and was an acknowledgement by the manufacturers (to be fair, acting on government instructions) of its many problems, as well as a plea to stick with it. In the event this was what happened – just – and the tank went on to acquire a fine service record. Among the man initial areas for concern were

Three of the Dieppe Mk Is were equipped with the TLC carpet device used to lay a canvas and wood trackway over the Chert pebbles of the beaches. The tanks carrying TLC were named BUTTERCUP, CHIEF, and this one is T68173 COUGAR of 13 Tp C Sqn.

The Bovington Tank Museum's Mk I – the 3" gun is a dummy as the tank is actually a Mk II with the BESA removed and replaced with a larger barrel. The tank was discovered in a bog in Yorkshire in the early 1980s; apparently it had been there since becoming booged in 1944! Painted to represent one of the Dieppe tanks, the overall colour should be SCC2 Brown, not the green used here, and the real BOB was actually a Mk III.

The Red-White-Red markings were the ground recognition symbols used to provide identification. The early small cast turret of the Mk I and II is a distinctive feature, which was found to be unsatisfactory and was replaced by a series of different designs from the Mk III onwards.

problems with the bogie wheels seizing, track link breakages, assorted leakages, parts shaking themselves loose, fuel supply and starvation issues, and unacceptably rapid clutch plate wear. In order to resolve these – and others – a novel approach was taken. Engineers were placed with the units receiving the tanks, in order to carry out two functions: to make sure that the crews understood the tank and its maintenance regimes, and to identify, report on, and where possible to rectify faults. This would ensure that the tanks were not being mishandled, and more importantly, ensure that the nature of all faults would be recorded and analysed with a view to rectification. Forced upon them because of the rush into production, it has to be said that this approach would commend itself to all new tanks, however extensively they had been trialled!

Again, in order to increase the output, additional firms were brought into the scheme, but with Vauxhall as the design parent – which meant the "owner" of the tank in terms of design and development. At least 10 firms contributed, although it must

The tank is fitted with a range of early features, including the heavy cast track links, which gave insufficient purchase on wet ground. However, the sheer thickness of the front armour plates can be appreciated from this view.

be said that many of them simply (do I really mean simply?) erected the tanks from components supplied from elsewhere, as opposed to firms who both made the parts and built tanks from them. The ones who made or erected Churchills were: Hartland & Wolff; Metro-Cammell; Birmingham Railway Carriage & Wagon; Dennis Brothers; Beyer-Peacock; Broom & Wade; Newton Chambers; Leyland; Gloucester Railway Carriage & Wagon; Charles Roberts.

The initial production mark was, unsurprisingly, the Mk I. Eventually eight main marks of tanks were made (plus some which were derivatives/conversions, ie the Mk IX onwards), as well as numerous special vehicles, including any number of

The driver's visor shown in the open position – the whole hinged plate could be opened when out of action to give the driver a better view, which was notoriously poor in the Churchill due to the protruding "horns" either side on the hull. The armoured glass prism has been painted over here.

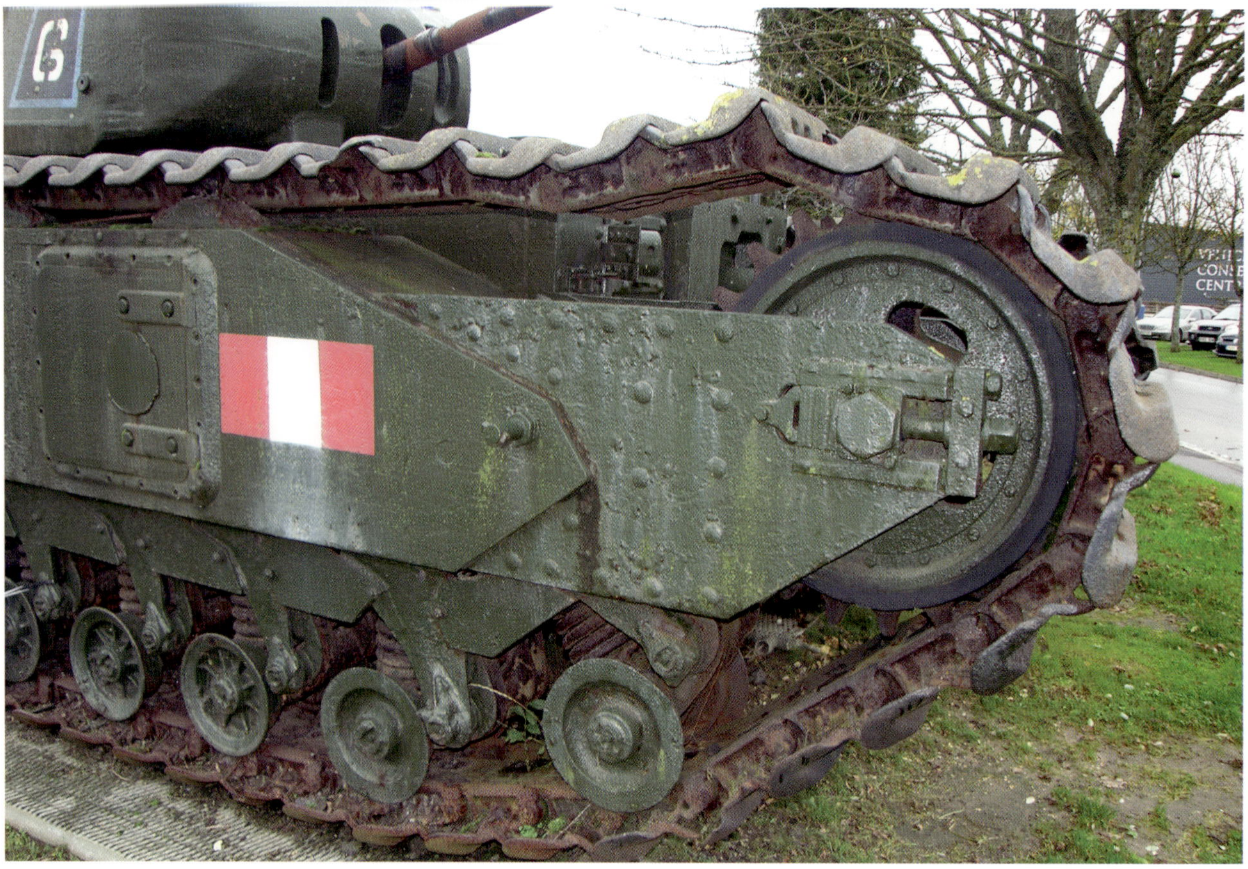

Mounted to the front of the hull is the idler wheel and track adjusting gear. Some of the eleven individually-mounted suspension units and small steel roadwheels can be seen.

The toothed idler wheel, an unusual design, as most idlers were plain wheels. It does however utilise rubber tyres which reduced the noise and to some extent, the vibration.

The early cast air intakes were not a good design as they tended to draw dust and debris off the ground into the engine, and were replaced during rework with a box design which drew the air in through mesh screens at the very top, and which were much easier to adapt for deep wading.

The rear of the hull is devoid of the many fittings that a service tank would have carried, but shows the actual width of the hull, made much wider by the side sponsons which carried the tracks and suspension.

The rectangular side hatch identifies a vehicle built originally as a Mk I to Mk VI. They were hinged to the front to provide extra protection from the likely angle of enemy fire, a sensible decision which saved a number of lives at Dieppe.

The pistol port on the right side of the turret rear, a standard feature on many British tanks. The thickness of the turret side armour can be gauged by the size of the "plug".

Another of the Kingforce tanks, camouflaged by applying Light Stone (or possibly Desert Pink) paint over the standard base colour. The canvas device in the front is a "dodger", designed to reduce the amount of dust at the front which would otherwise obscure the driver's vision.

bridgelayers, engineer assault vehicles or AVREs, armoured recovery tanks (ARV), and flamethrowers (known as Crocodiles). The main features of each mark were as follows:

- Mk I: small cast turret, 2 pounder gun. 3" howitzer in hull mount. No trackguards. Square escape hatches on hull. (In instances where the guns were swapped over, the tank was referred to as a Mk I CS)
- Mk II: small cast turret, 3" howitzer. BESA MG in hull mount. No trackguards
- Mk III: welded turret, 6 pounder gun. Full trackguards
- Mk IV: larger cast turret, 6 pounder gun. (Tanks with the US M3 75mm gun fitted inti a modified turret were called NA75)
- Mk V: larger cast turret, 95mm gun.

The Kingforce Churchills were modified to take the Sunshield device, which is shown here. The attention to detail on the front is high, especially the depiction of the lorry driver's windscreen with typical clear wiper area.

- Mk VI: larger cast turret, similar to Mk IV but with 75mm gun.
- Mk VII: new cast/welded turret, 75mm gun. Increased hull armour (max 152mm) Circular escape hatches on hull
- Mk VIII: as Mk VII with 95mm gun.

This diagram illustrates the hits sustained by Lt Peter Gudgin's Churchill described by him in the text. Because he was able to inspect the tank later, he could accurately describe the calibre of each shot, rather than – as many did – claim that they were all from eighty-eights!

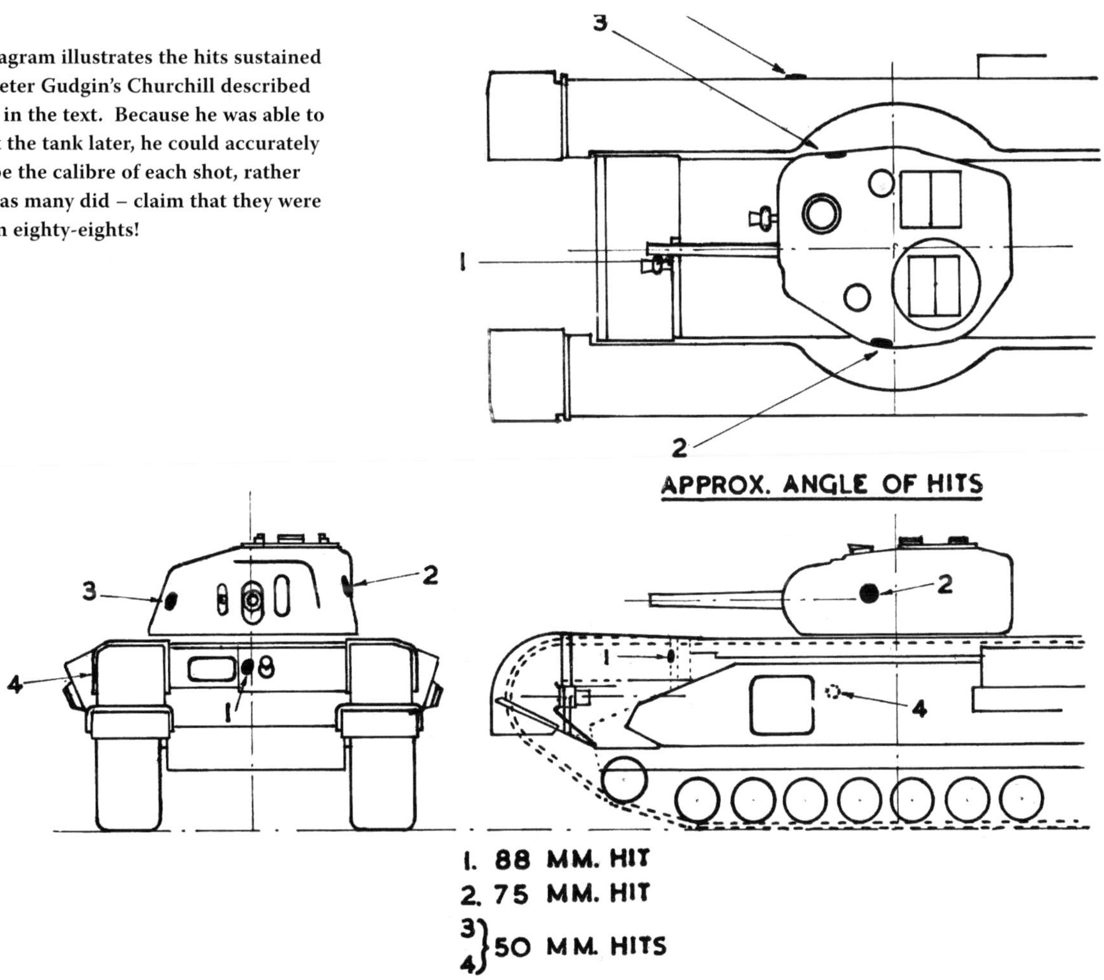

- Mk IX: Mk III or IV with appliqué armour on hull (to 152mm) and turret to Mk VII standard, heavy suspension
- Mk IXLT: as Mk IX but with normal turret (LT stood for Light Turret, meaning the original turret with no applique armour)
- Mk X: Mk VI with appliqué armour on hull and turret to Mk VII standard, heavy suspension
- Mk XLT: as Mk X but with normal turret
- Mk XI: with appliqué armour on hull and turret to Mk VII standard, heavy suspension
- Mk XILT: as Mk XI but with normal turret

With the Churchill, identifying marks, and even production, is a notoriously difficult procedure, due to the extensive re-working programme that was necessary after the initial dramas when it was introduced into service. Many tanks built as one mark were almost completely re-built to a later specification, and there is even the possibility that some were upgraded more than once! So it is entirely possible for a Mk I tank to be re-built to Mk III standard, and then later to Mk IV. Additionally, the selection of tanks for re-working was not always done in batches, so it is possible to note three tanks built on the same initial production run with consecutive registration numbers, but all three ending up as different marks! Additionally, suffix letters (A, B, C, R, X etc) were often added to the registration in order to clarify the exact state of modification. The production table used here must therefore be taken with a degree of caution, as it is a combination of the official census (registration) lists, the individual contract cards, unit records, and the interpretation of photographs. The marks shown are those of the original build. It seems that around 5222 Churchills were built over a four year period.

Although the Churchill could take a lot of punishment, it was never invulnerable. This Mk III was photographed in Normandy after being hit by 88mm AP on the side applique armour, which caused the crew to bale out but they were all unharmed.

A Mk III in Soviet service, complete with winter camouflage and soviet insignia on the turret.

REGISTRATIONS	QUANTITY	QTY	MAKER
T10418 – T10421	I	4	H&W
T30971 – T31272	I, II, III & IV	302	VAUXHALL
T31322 – T31420	III & IV	99	VAUXHALL
T31421 – T31495	I, II, III & IV	75	DENNIS
T31496 – T31670	I, II, III & IV	175	METRO-CAMMELL
T31671 – T31745	III	75	BEYER PEACOCK
T31746 – T31820	I, II, III & IV	75	BROOM & WADE
T31821 – T31994	I, II, III & IV	174	BRCW
T31996 – T32070	I, II, III & IV	75	NEWTON CHAMBERS
T32071 – T32145	I, II, III & IV	74	H&W
T32144 – T32395	I, II, III & IV	250	LEYLAND
T32396 – T32470	I, II, III & IV	75	GRCW
T67867 – T68140	III & IV	274	VAUXHALL
T68141 – T68440	III	300	VAUXHALL
T68441 – T68584	I, II, III & IV	144	VAUXHALL
T68585 – T68640	III & IV	55	VAUXHALL
T68641 – T69140	I, II, III & IV	500	VAUXHALL
T172001 – T172101	III & IV	329	NEWTON CHAMBERS
T172102 – T172329	III & IV	228	LEYLAND
T172330 – T172379	III & IV	50	DENNIS
T172380 – T172479	III & IV	100	NEWTON CHAMBERS
T172480 – T172529	III & IV	50	GRCW
T172530 – T172579	III & IV	50	CHARLES ROBERTS
T251505 – T251667	VII & VIII	163	VAUXHALL
T251668 – T251880	IV, V & VI	213	VAUXHALL
T251881 – T252504	III, IV, V, VI & VII	621	VAUXHALL
T331700	VI	1	VAUXHALL
T341209 – T341308	VII	100	NOT KNOWN
T341309 – T341408	VII	100	DENNIS
T341409 – T341508	VII	100	GRCW
T341509 – T341608	VII	100	VAUXHALL
T341609 – T341708	VIII	100	NEWTON CHAMBERS
T347659 – T347848	VII & VIII	190	VAUXHALL
T347848	VII	1	VAUXHALL

Over time, the Churchill became increasingly popular with its crew, despite its antediluvian appearance and its dreadful introduction into service. This was partly because its mechanical unreliability was solved, but primarily because it was very heavily armoured, with the front hull plates of the early marks being 4" (102mm) thick, which was then increased to 6" (152mm)

A crewman from the 3rd Armoured Bn Scots Guards stands in front of his 95mm armed CS Mk V around autumn 1944. Many units chose to attach what they thought of as extra armour in the form of track links to both hull and turret, but in reality it added next to no protection at the expense of a lot of additional weight.

The turret of this Churchill was displaced off the turret ring after being hit by a large calibre HE impact, which also split the 6 Pounder barrel. (The item on the turret roof is a Thermos jar, part of the tool kit.)

A Churchill III being carried by an ally – in the shape of an American M25 Dragon wagon, comprising an M26 armoured tractor and an M15 40 ton trailer. The location of the photograph is not known, but the attitudes of the soldiers and the lack of equipment on the tank appears to make it a training exercise.

Churchill III T32203R was a reworked Churchill made by Leyland, the R suffix denoting the fact that it has been rebuilt into the Mk III configuration; as well as the fording height instructions, she also carries the typical and commonplace coolant instructions stencilled onto the rear trackguard. She is armed with the long-barrelled early 6 Pounder gun, and is being loaded onto an M15 trailer by US Army crews.

The AVRE version of the Churchill was one of the very successful Funnies, and fired a spigot HEAT projectile used to demolish bunkers, obstacles and the like. Reloading the weapon had to be done by the co-driver, an unenviable task!

The Mk VII was the last and best gun tank version built. Armed with a 75mm gun, it was sometimes called the A22F, or alternatively the Heavy Churchill, as it mounted up to 6" of armour on the hull front, making it very difficult to penetrate.

This Mk V armed with a 95mm gun has the diamond marking on the turret, telling us that it is serving within a Regimental Headquarters (RHQ) troop. T173254B is shown here in Australian service, who subsequently converted it into an Armoured Recovery Vehicle (ARV)

Churchill as propaganda! Although no Churchills are thought to have been used against Japanese forces, it has not stopped an artist from using a Mk III as inspiration for this poster.

One of the most feared and hated variants used was the Crocodile, the flamethrower variant. It towed a trailer containing the fuel, which was passed underneath and then into the front of the hull, where the normal BESA MG was replaced by the flame device. Some crews preferred to 'demonstrate' its use in an attempt to persuade enemies to surrender before the weapon was turned on them.

on the Mk VII and VII, the so-called Heavy Churchill; this was more than on the front of the majority of the German tanks, including Tiger 1. British studies of knocked-out vehicles during the Normandy campaign gave clear statistical evidence to demonstrate the value of this. Over half of all AP hits on the Churchill failed to penetrate, and the majority of hits on the thickest plates failed to damage the tank. When this is compared to the Sherman where over 70% of AP hits did penetrate, it can be appreciated how good the Churchill was. Additionally, the tank did not "brew up" anything like as quickly as other types, giving the crew extra time to escape. These qualities were apparent as soon as the tank was used in action, both during the attack on Dieppe in August 1942 (its debut) and then in North Africa from October 1942 onwards. By the time it was being extensively used in Tunisia in 1943, its armour plus an amazingly ability to climb steep hills were both widely praised. An example from 21st April 1943 tells an interesting tale. Lt Peter Gudgin was commanding a Churchill Mk IV in 4 Troop, A Squadron

The threat from magnetic mines caused the Germans to paste Zimmerit onto their tanks. The British experimented with a similar covering, known as AMCO or anti magnetic mine coating and shown here on a Mk VII. It was not a success.

T252107/H was built by Vauxhall and used for a number of trials, including the AMCO test shown earlier. Here it is fitted with plywood, representing spaced armour. This was fitted by the Department of Tank Design at Chertsey in December 1944, who were assessing whether skirting plates, as much used by the Germans, could be fitted to Churchill without getting in the way of the tanks ability to fight.

48RTR. He wrote a description of being knocked out based on his recollections but also, unusually, he then had the chance to examine his tank later when it was being repaired in workshops:

> *I received 4 hits from German A/Tk guns of various calibres. Hits 2, 3 and 4 occurred practically simultaneously, about ten seconds after hit 1. The crew commenced to bail out immediately after the first hit, but were not clear before the last three. Hit 1. An 88mm shot hit the co-driver's MG mounting, penetrated and passed down the length of the tank into the engine. En route, it set off four rounds of 6 Pounder ammunition in unarmoured clips behind the driver and started a fire in the engine compartment. [This fire] was extinguished by the CO2 bottle but later re-ignited by ammunition fire. The*

T252107/H was built by Vauxhall and used for a number of trials, including the AMCO test shown earlier. Here it is fitted with plywood, representing spaced armour. This was fitted by the Department of Tank Design at Chertsey in December 1944, who were assessing whether skirting plates, as much used by the Germans, could be fitted to Churchill without getting in the way of the tanks ability to fight.

T 252107/H

Circular side doors are one of the giveaway features owf the A22F heavy Churchill, so-called because of the additional weight of armour carried. This is the right hand side.

A suspension unit photographed after being unbolted from the tank. Although quite crude, with no rubber on the wheels, they were easily removed and replaced if damaged, particularly by mines. With eleven units either side, of which nine were in contact with the ground, the tank could afford to have two or more damaged and still be able to drive, provide that the tracks were intact.

tank stopped; the driver and co-driver were the only members of the crew affected by this round, and commenced to bail out. Hit 2. A 75mm shot hit the left hand side of the turret at approximately 45° to normal, beside the Commander, but did not penetrate. Petals of armour, however, set off a 6 Pdr round which had been placed in grenade rack (the grenades having been removed.) Of this I am certain because I was beside the round when it went off. Hit 3. One 50mm shot hit the right hand front of the turret ring, stuck in the armour with its nose just through, and set off the 2" smoke ammunition. I know this happened immediately after impact because I smelt the different smoke. Hit 4. Another 50mm shot hit the right hand side plate behind the escape hatch at approximately 45° to normal, did not completely penetrate, but flaking inside set off several rounds near the operator. Casualties: Driver – burned. Co-Driver – one arm and three ribs broken and burned. Operator – splinters in leg, one arm broken by hit on turret. Gunner – slightly burned on back, splinters in leg. Commander – blinded by flash, splinters in legs.

The Churchill went on to serve extensively in Italy, where its lack of speed was much less important than its armour and hill-climbing ability. The nature of the terrain and enemy defensive tactics meant that HE ammunition was used much more than AP, hence the need for 75mm armed tanks, as the 6 Pounder was a good hole-puncher but lacked explosive power in its HE round. This was initially met by the conversion of a number of tanks to mount the American M3 75mm gun, the mounting and mantlets taken from Shermans, the so-called NA (for North Africa) 75. Later marks equipped with the British 75mm gun, essentially a re-bored 6 Pounder, made the NA75 redundant. Churchill – and variants – was used throughout the slow campaign to liberate Italy, and it could almost have been made for the job, becoming extremely popular with its crews.

It was in Northern Europe that the Churchill really cemented its reputation. Its first appearance in that theatre was as part of the Dieppe raid of August 1942, when 29 Mk I and III Churchills supported the landings, operated by 14th Canadian Army Tank Regiment, better known as the Calgary Regiment. Although all the tanks that disembarked were lost in the action, they did not "fail to clear the beach" as some accounts state; rather, they did, but could not penetrate into the town due to barricades that reconnaissance had failed to spot. Although badly mauled by the German guns, their protection once again was praised by the crews, although the Germans do seem to have been bemused by their analysis of the captured vehicles. Indeed, it seems that they believed that the Churchills were used on the raid simply because they were poorly designed and could therefore be sacrificed at Dieppe!

The Germans would learn the error of this assumption when they next encountered them in Northern Europe, on 6th June 1944. Having learned from Dieppe that it was not feasible to seize a port by coup de main, and having solved the early reliability problems by this stage, the British army supported its landings in Normandy with a whole range of specialised armoured variants of Churchills known as the Funnies, and

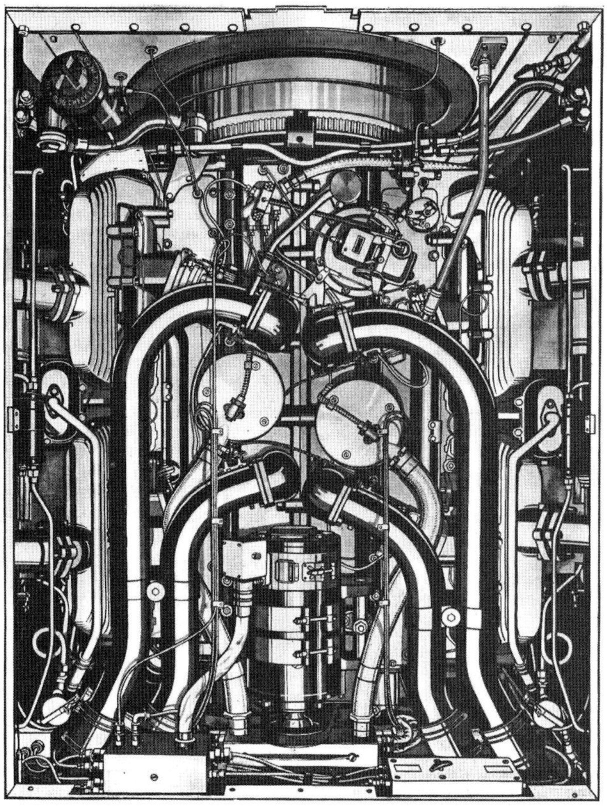

The engine bay seen from the top, with the various leads, cables and pipes shown

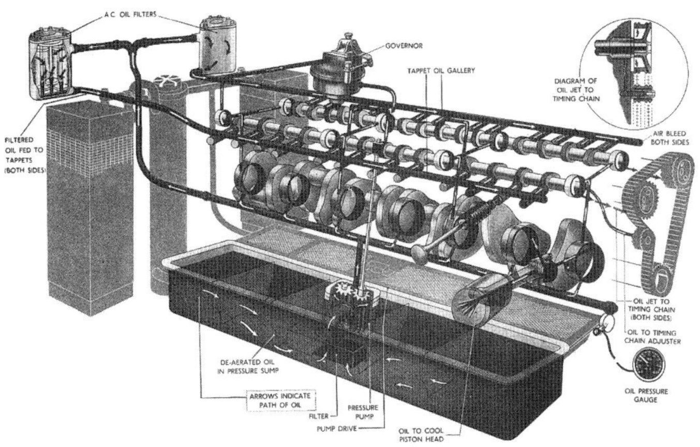

Perspective diagram of engine lubrication—PRESSURE system.

Inside the engine, this diagram shows the lubrication system within the engine.

The engine used on all the Churchill marks was a Bedford Twin-Six 350 bhp petrol unit. This was a 12 cylinder engine that gave a top speed of only around 16 mph on a road, and about half that across country. But of course as an infantry tank more speed was not specified!

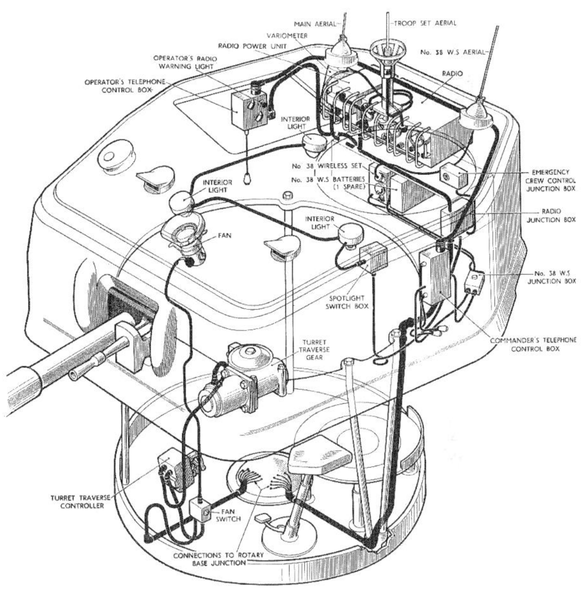

Diagram of turret wiring layout—Churchill VIII.

The electrical components within the Mk VIII turret, with the reliable No 19 set on the rear sill, and the radio harness boxes which allowed each of the three turret crewmen to communicate. Note that it is also fitted with a separate No 38 radio, used to communicate with the infantry.

which were designed to breach specific types of obstacles. These are widely acknowledged to have played a key role in ensuring the success of the initial lodgement, and in assisting further by providing assault and obstacle support for the rest of the campaign. By 1944 the Churchill VII variant was in the hands of troops; this was armed with a useful dual-purpose 75mm gun, and carried even more armour that the earlier marks (which had the same frontal protection as the Tiger 1), mounting no less than 152mm (6") on the front, as well as additional armour mounted on the hull sides and turret. The utility of the Funnies can be realised by the fact that at the end of hostilities in 1945, the Royal Armoured Corps rapidly shrank and disposed of much of its wartime equipment, especially the older designs. However, the need for specialist AFVs – bridges, flamethrowers, ARV, AVRE and the like – in any future conflicts was clear to all, and many Churchill variants were retained on the strength. Indeed, Churchill's final battle proved to be in Korea, when C Sqn 7RTR was deployed to Pusan in November 1950 to assist with the repulsion of the invasion there. This unit was equipped with Crocodile flamethrowers, based on a tank first designed ten years before and which was nearly scrapped early in its development because of its poor reputation!

Conclusion

Despite the fact that the artificial division of tanks into different classes for different roles was proved to be false during the war, because the battlefield did not oblige itself by providing neat distinctions, three of the four Infantry tanks that Britain put into service must be judged as broadly successful. The Matilda II provided its crews with a level of armour pro-

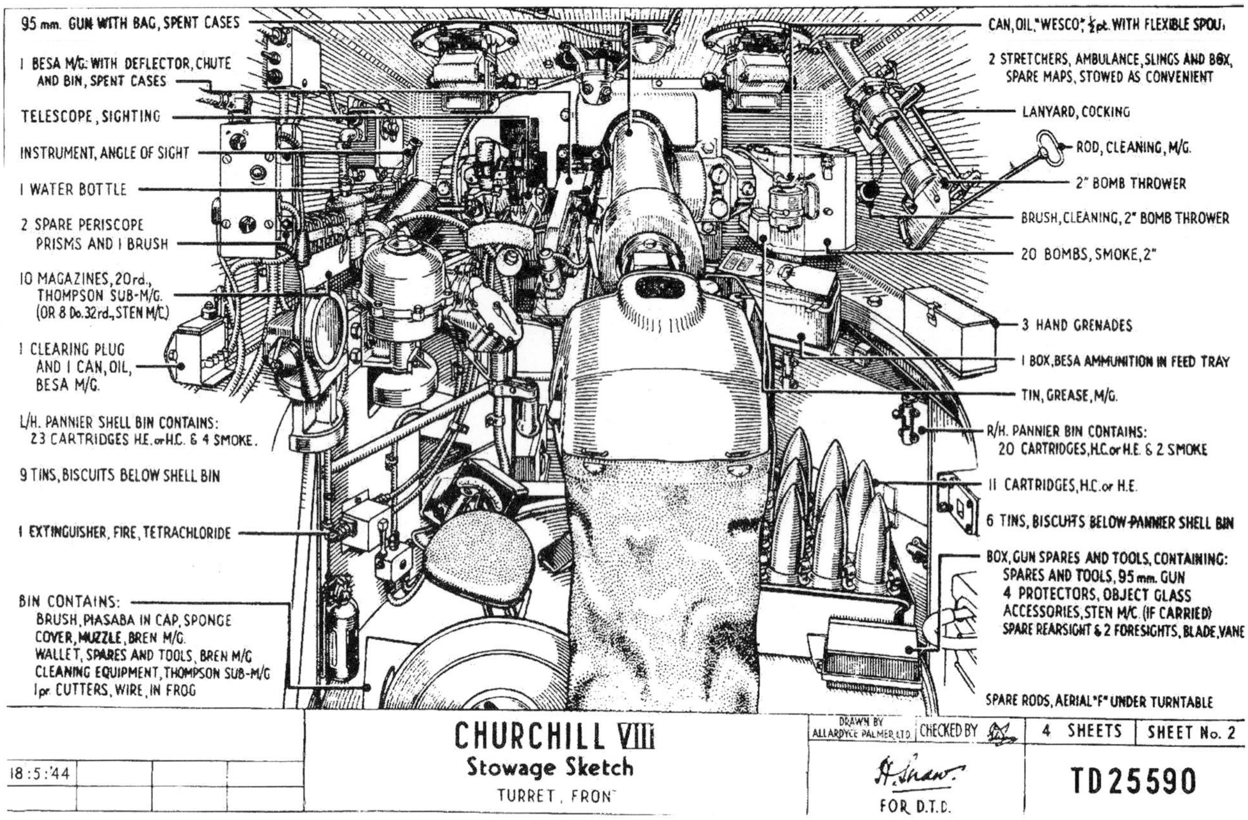

A stowage sketch showing the layout and tool and ammunition stowage within the Mk VIII turret. The 2" smoke bomb thrower which projected through the turret roof is to the right of the 95mm gun.

tection that for a year or so rendered it just about immune to frontal attacks from the standard anti-tank guns of the day. It briefly enjoyed the same sort of respect that the Tiger was to achieve later, albeit without the powerful armament to back up its armour credentials. Even when it was obsolete in Europe, it was used by the fledgling Australian armoured corps in the Pacific, giving the infantry much-needed close support. The Valentine was small, simple and mechanically

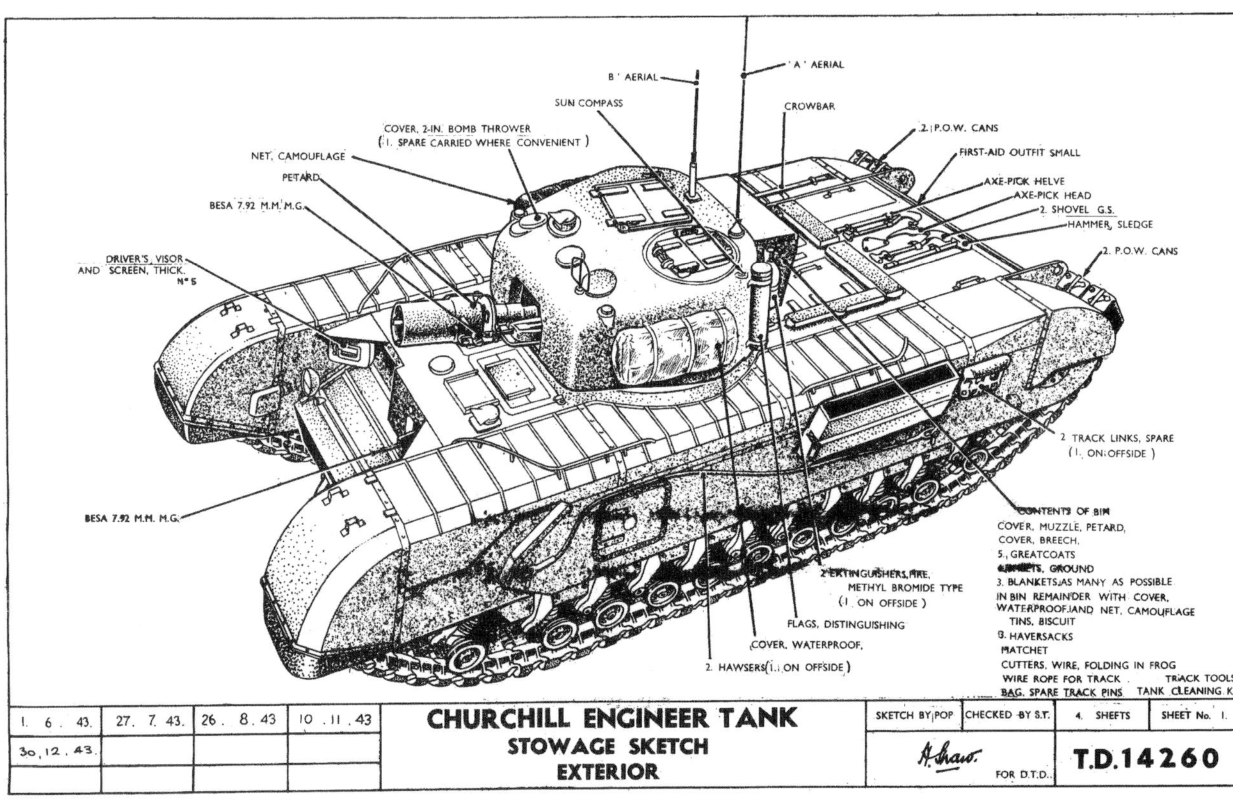

External stowage; the Mk VII was similar, the difference being the special tools carried for either the 75mm or the 95mm gun (marked here as "Petard").

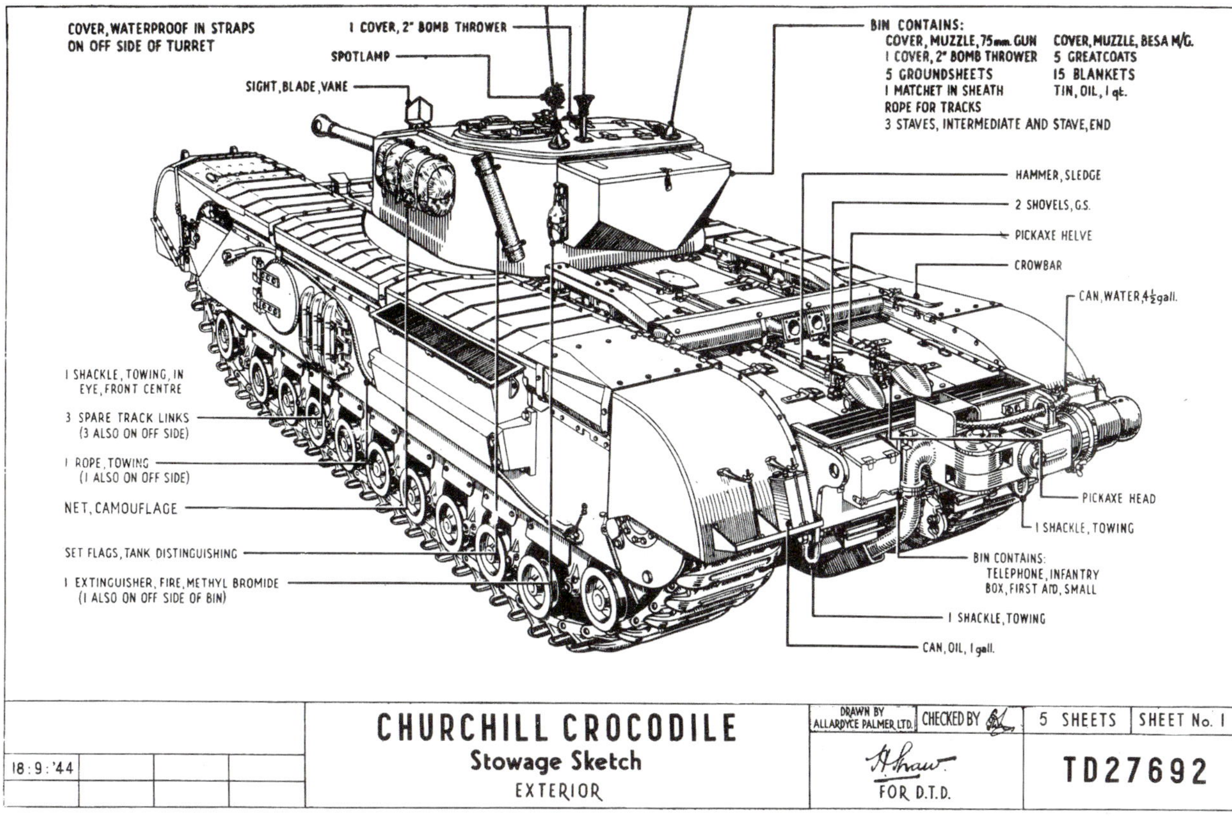

Crocodile stowage from the rear, without the fuel trailer being shown. The complicated linkage is however detailed, and shows how the fuel mixture was fed underneath the belly of the tank.

reliable, and was produced in more numbers than any other British tank. It allowed the Canadian industry to learn how to construct tanks for the first time, and it also found favour with the Russian crews who used it up right until the end of the war. Mounting only just adequate armour, it was capable of being up-gunned to prolong its life, and its role as the DD training tank was invaluable. The best of the bunch was the Churchill, whose terrible rushed entry into service was caused by the circumstances of the time. Once the problem of reliability was solved, it took its crews into battle as the Allied tank which gave them the best chances of survival if they were hit. It too was successfully up-gunned, and it formed the basis of a family of specialised armoured vehicles that proved to be a crucial factor on D-Day and beyond. The ugly duckling (pun intended) of the four was the first of the I-Tank line, the unlovely and unloved Matilda I, built down to a price and which not surprisingly failed to deliver, but still managed to give the German army a nasty shock at Arras mainly due to its unusually thick armour. So all played their part to a greater or lesser degree, and we must remember that over 16,000 of them were built and most were used in action, testament to their utility as well as to the doctrine of the day.

Although it may look like one at first glance, this is not a Churchill at all, but a proposed Super-Churchill called A43 Black Prince. Mounting the excellent 17 Pounder gun, 6 prototypes were made before the project was cancelled.

A surviving Churchill Mk III AVRE, clearly demonstrating the applique armour welded onto the turret and hull, to bring the tank up to the same standards as the heavy Churchill. The badge on the front is that of 79th Armoured Division, who operated the "Funnies".

One of the Tank Museum's three A11s is in running order and is seen here as a walkaround. On the left side of the turret is one of the pair of 4" smoke bomb throwers, which used a cable-operated modified .303" rifle.

The driver's visor was closed in action, but allowed the driver to operate with his head out at other times.

This early Matilda I features the high-mounted headlamps, and the early simple form of vision slit for the driver.

Tools were mounted externally on brackets along the hull sides, and include one of the Pyrene fire extinguishers.

This image shows the problem of the driver's visor – when in action, trying to raise it when the gun was over the front caused an obstruction, making it difficult for the driver to escape easily. The aerial base fitted here is a post-war type, and is not representative of the dome type used with the No 11 radio set.

The .303" Vickers MMG was mounted in an armoured cowl, designed to prevent the water jacket that cooled the barrel from being punctured in action. The water jacket was fed from a reservoir mounted inside the turret.

The towing cable was coiled and stowed alongside the hull. If a tank required towing, the cables from both could be used. The metal plate stowed behind the tow rope (another one is fitted to the opposite side) is used to blank-off the air intake louvres for the engine, causing air to be drawn instead through the internal bulkhead, and creating a very unpleasant draught for the crew!

The sloping rear decks for the Ford engine and at the rear, the transmission. Air was normally drawn in through the front two grilles, and released to atmosphere out of the two at the rear. Note the starting handle stowed on the side.

The exhaust pipe and silencer on the right rear of the engine was quite exposed, but there was no room inside the compartment for it.

More stowage on the rear of the hull, in the form of two wooden jacking blocks, plus the jack. It is not clear where the jack handle was stowed, as it is not mentioned on the stowage diagrams, so it may have been placed in one of the two kit bins.

Although four jacking blocks are shown here, two larger blocks were more commonly carried.

To allow the tank to be recovered in action, and also to be lashed down when being transported by train etc, the rear of the hull has two large shackles, one either side of the final drive drums.

At the front of the suspension are the track adjuster mechanisms. These worked on a ratchet principle, allowing track tension to be increased when the track stretched in use.

Rudimentary track guards were fitted at the front and rear, but not over the track runs in the middle.

The adjustment mechanisms were simple but effective, although it can be appreciated just how exposed they were to damage, from shellfire, mines etc.

At the rear of the hull the sprocket wheels that drive the tracks are to be found, protruding from the final drive drums.

The suspension units, including shock absorbing springs and roadwheels, were based on those used with the Dragon Mk IV artillery tractor. The rearmost pair of wheels did not have rubber tyres, as these were found to disintegrate very easily.

The top of the small cast turret, showing the two hatches for the commander, and the housing for the single Vickers tank periscope mounted for use when closed down

The cast turret from the rear right marked up as a 4RTR vehicle (which the museum example was not), with the unit's Chinese Eye symbol and the two colour 1940 camouflage scheme.

The mechanism for raising and lowering the driver's visor was by means of the rotating handle shown here. The very simple instrument panel is also shown. The remainder of the hull fittings here are modern, and do not accurately replicate the wartime vehicle.

The traversing handle for the turret has been roped off to prevent it traversing. Elevation and depression of the Vickers MMG was by means of a shoulder pad, designed to allow shooting on the move.

The left-hand of the two visor handles, which could be raised or lowered very quickly. Driving closed-down using the periscope or the vision slits must have been an uncomfortable and difficult task.

Inside the gearbox compartment, with the linkages shown. The simplicity of the vehicle made it easy to maintain and repair, which added to its reliability.

The semi-circular cover fitted into the transmission compartment hatch is to allow the use of the PTO for the Fowler mineplough, and was a feature of the second type of A11.

One of the Tank Museum's examples survived despite being used as a hard target on a range! Its 60mm armour proved capable of resisting a lot of the shots fired at it, although some of the larger calibres got through. In 1940 however, such ammunition was not readily available, as the German's soon discovered.

Two penetrations close together at the top have caused the armour to crack, but there are at least four “scoops” visible where the shot has been deflected.

The other side of the turret is in good condition, as it was facing away from the guns on the range. The bracket for one of the smoke bomb throwers can be seen.

A great view of the ‘business end’ of the turret, showing the amount of protection afforded to the Vickers MMG by the armoured cowl. The gun was offset to the right slightly, to allow the commander to fire the gun using the shoulder piece in his right shoulder.

The toothed sprocket and rings with the track removed, which allows a clear view of the final drive casing.

The rear right pf the hull rear, with the mounting bracket for the towing shackle.

The A11 used the same armour basis all round, an impressive 60mm. This was made up of plates riveted together, the three main hull plates being shown here.

The mounting brackets for the idler wheel and track adjusting gear. Although it looks crude, it had to be if the cost was to be kept down

The mounting brackets for the idler wheel and track adjusting gear. Although it looks crude, it had to be if the cost was to be kept down.

The mounting brackets for the idler wheel and track adjusting gear. Although it looks crude, it had to be if the cost was to be kept down.

The idler wheel on the prototype was toothed, but was replaced by a simpler plain cast wheel on the production tanks.

Because the tank was so small, changing and repairing individual components would have been a simple task for the crew and RAOC mechanics, certainly much easier that was to come as tanks got larger and heavier.

The mounting brackets for the suspension units were bolted onto the hull sides; the stub-axle used to support the units and allow them to pivot is very obvious.

The number of rivets needed to make up the hull from its individual components was large, and as well as adding weight, they proved to be a weak point, as a direct hit on one could cause it to be fired into the inside of the tank, injuring the crew and damaging components.

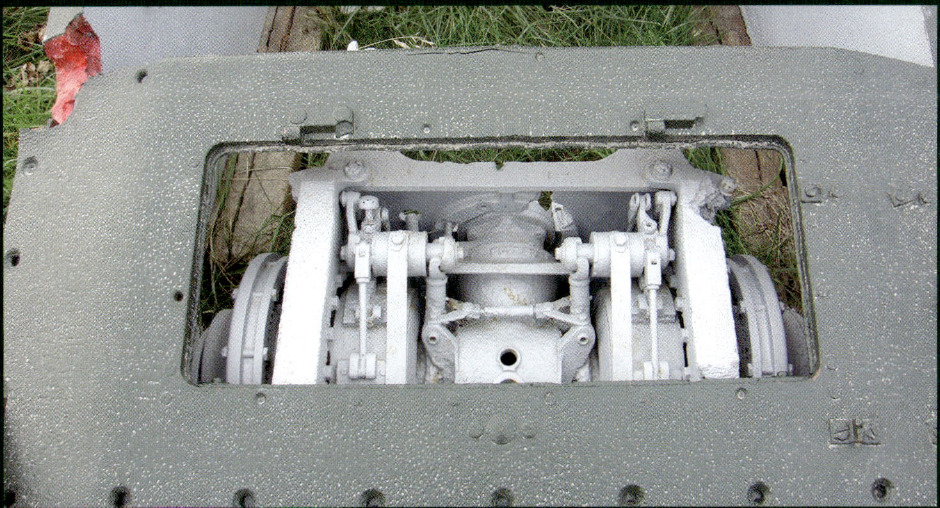

The view from the rear looking forwards: the pointed nose still contains the stowage boxes used to hold spare armoured prisms for his emergency lookout, which can be seen on the vertical plate.

With the visor closed, if the tank periscope was damaged the driver would resort to looking out through the four slits of his emergency lookout, which was protected by an armoured glass prism to help prevent bullet splash hitting him.

The left side of the driver's compartment would have mounted his gas mask and the commander's signal pistol in its leather holster.

Looking to the rear, the toothed connection from the (missing) engine into the gearbox is visible, as are the internal conical heads for the

This A11 was probably a later model, as it features the pivoting armoured (and ballistically shaped) cover for the emergency lookout, a similar design to that used on the Valentine.

A 50p piece measures about 28mm across, which was twice the standard thickness of armour used when the A11 was conceived. Providing it with 60mm of armour proved to be the saving grace, making the tank incredibly well-armoured for the day, and saving the lives of many soldiers during its short service life.

The PTO for the mineplough fitted to the transmission hatch is a give-away feature of later production vehicles.

A typical brass vehicle identification plate, giving not only the military registration of T8106, but also the month of manufacture. 2635 is probably the manufacturer's reference number.

Painted by Arkadiusz Wróbel

When Matilda I was first produced they were painted in an overall semi-gloss single colour called Deep Bronze Green, which is shown here, typical of a tank when first built in the UK. This was the standard colour used for much of the 1930s, until it was replaced in May 1938 with a more suitable matt colour known as Khaki Green No 3. At this time the tanks wore both the civilian registration number (HMH789) and their census number starting with T (T3434). This tank was produced around August 1938 and was probably the first Matilda I to be handed over to a field unit.

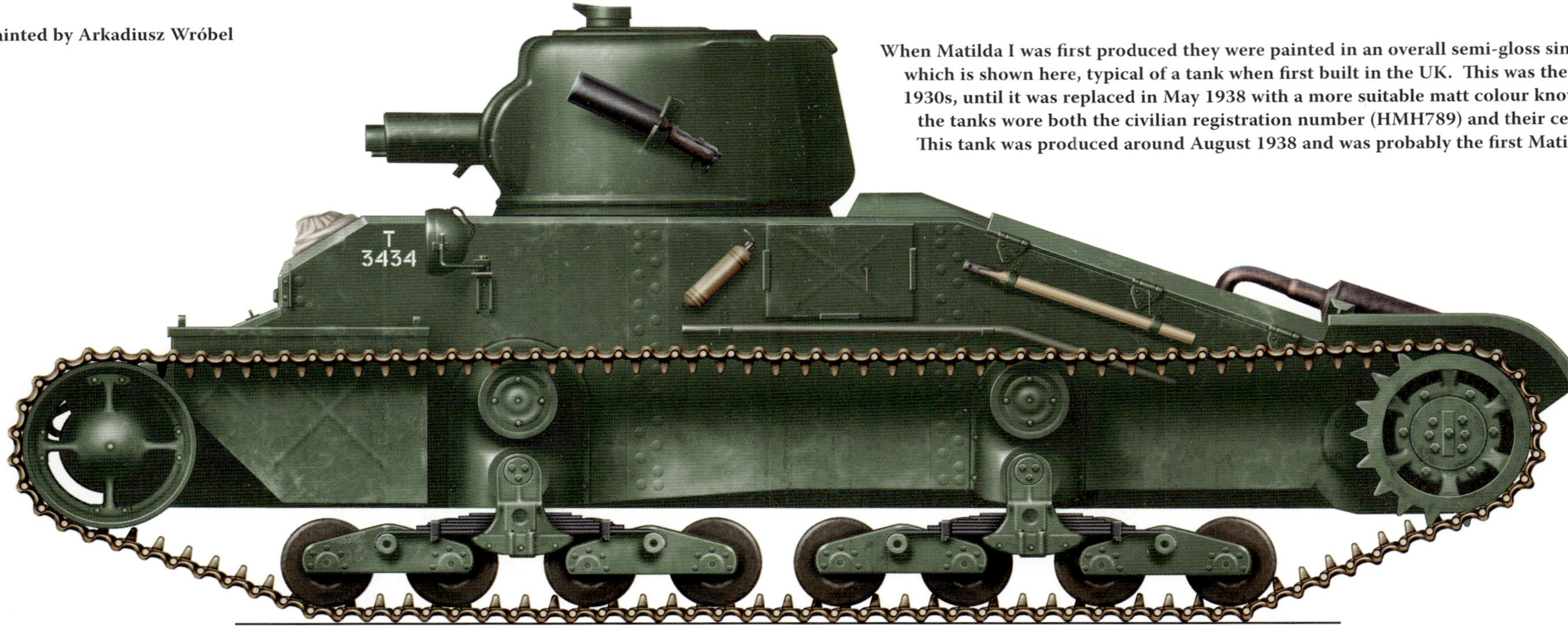

This Matilda is wearing the so-called MTP 20 Scheme 1, consisting over a base coat of Green G3 overpainted with an irregular pattern of darker green G4 stripes. This is the scheme that the tanks of 1st Army Tank Brigade went to France wearing in late 1939. The white rectangle is the recognition symbol. This tank belongs to 4RTR, as it has the Chinese Eyes of that regiment on the turret, and the name – DEVIL – starts with a D.

Painted by Arkadiusz Wróbel

A Matilda II captured by the Germans at Bir Hakeim in 1942 and wearing an unusual camouflage scheme. Although the colours are not known, a study of the photographs indicates that it may be a green or brown shade over the usual Light Stone. It is probably a British design, as the "artists" have attempted to include the outline of wheels for use with the Sunshade device. The colour of the turret number is likewise unknown, but is shown here in white and red for contrast.

T18858 was a Mk IN Matilda II produced by Ruston & Hornsby. Following service in a British unit (it still has an A Sqn triangle on the side along with the fording markings) it was sent to the USSR in April 1942, where it was captured after serving with 194 Tank Brigade – the 24 on the turret front and rear are Russian markings. Due to the desperate situation in the USSR at this time, the Soviets would not have had the time or inclination to repaint these tanks, hence it has remained in SCC2 with its British markings.

Painted by Arkadiusz Wróbel

T1290281 is a typical Valentine Mk IV, in use by Polish armoured forces training in Scotland. The Poles were allocated their own range of census (registration) numbers, from 1288563 to 1293562 when the vehicles were transferred across from the British army. Note the large PL sign denoting its nationality; these were often marked on the rear as well.

The 11th Armoured Division formed in UK in February 1941, and were equipped with Valentines as there were insufficient Cruiser tanks for them to train with. This Valentine was used by the junior armoured regiment in the second armoured brigade, the Westminster Dragoons.

Painted by Arkadiusz Wróbel

SHEPHERD was a Churchill I of 1 Troop B Sqn 43RTR in August 1942. At that time the regiment was the senior unit of 33rd Tank Brigade in the 3rd Infantry Division in southern England, therefore the squadron and troop insignia on the turret are painted in red. The Red-White-Red recognition insignia is used on all four sides of the hull, including on the fuel drum on the rear. On the front plate, in addition to the recognition rectangle in the centre, are the Class 40 bridge marking, the 3rd Infantry Division sign (devised by Montgomery), and the Arm of Service number 67. Overall the tank is painted in SCC2 Brown, introduced in late 1941 and which was the main colour used in Europe for the middle years of the war. T32314 was made by Leyland, and after serving with 43RTR was passed to Welbeck College.

T30974 was a Vauxhall-built Mk 1 used by B Sqn 9RTR as a training tank in UK in early 1943. At that time, 9RTR was the second senior regiment in the 31st Tank Brigade, and thus used yellow tactical markings, although it did not use troop numbers within the shapes as most units did – rather, it used the very large tank names for recognition purposes. (Presumably, everyone either learned the names or carried a list!)

ICENI is a Churchill III of 2 Tp, C Sqn 9RTR in August 1944; notice how the tank names are now painted in a much smaller font. After moving to Normandy with 31st Tank Brigade, in September the regiment switched across to 34th Tank Brigade where it remained for the rest of the war. When in 31st TB the unit was the second senior regiment, using yellow markings as shown here, but on moving to 34th TB it became the senior regiment and had to repaint everything red to denote its new status. Notice also how the SCC2 brown has darkened with age and service.

Painted by Arkadiusz Wróbel

Tanks of 21st Tank Brigade in Tunisia in 1943 applied a striped camouflage pattern over the SCC2 of their tanks, in an attempt to blend in with the surroundings. Although the lighter colour might be the new "Light Mud" paint being introduced at that time ready for the Italian campaign, most accounts indicate that the crews simply mixed up real mud and applied that over their vehicles, which would account for the scruffy finish seen in photographs. This obliterated most of the markings used, although this Churchill III of 145 Regiment RAC has taken care to leave the blue C Squadron circle on the turret bin visible; the Red-White-Red recognition sign on the hull rears were also left clean.

PHOTOSNIPER 3D
20
PANZER IV
AUSF. H AND AUSF. J
Łukasz Gładysiak, Samir Karmieh
vol. I
KAGERO
Buy now
Photosniper
Panzer IV – vol. I, vol. II
PHOTOSNIPER 3D
22
PANZER IV
AUSF. H AND AUSF. J
Łukasz Gładysiak, Samir Karmieh
vol. II
KAGERO
shop.kagero.pl • shop.kagero.pl • shop.ka

KAGERO MINIATURES
MINIATURES COLLECTION 1/32
RESIN PARTS FOR ASSEMBLY AND PAINTINGS